The Development of Western Civilization

*Narrative Essays in the History of Our Tradition from
Its Origins in Ancient Israel and Greece to the Present*

Edited by Edward W. Fox
*Professor of Modern European History
Cornell University*

MEDIAEVAL SOCIETY

By SIDNEY PAINTER

Mediaeval Society

SIDNEY PAINTER

Cornell University Press

ITHACA AND LONDON

STANDARD BOOK NUMBER 8014-9850-3

PRINTED IN THE UNITED STATES OF AMERICA BY THE

VAIL-BALLOU PRESS, INC., BINGHAMTON, NEW YORK

Foreword

THE proposition that each generation must rewrite history is more widely quoted than practiced. In the field of college texts on western civilization, the conventional accounts have been revised, and sources and supplementary materials have been developed; but it is too long a time since the basic narrative has been rewritten to meet the rapidly changing needs of new college generations. In the mid-twentieth century such an account must be brief, well written, and based on unquestioned scholarship and must assume almost no previous historical knowledge on the part of the reader. It must provide a coherent analysis of the development of western civilization and its basic values. It must, in short, constitute a systematic introduction to the collective memory of that tradition which we are being asked to defend. This series of narrative essays was undertaken in an effort to provide such a text for an introductory history survey course and is being published in the present form in the belief that the requirements of that one course reflected a need that is coming to be widely recognized.

Now that the classic languages, the Bible, the great historical novels, even most non-American history, have dropped out of the normal college preparatory program, it is imperative that a text in the history of European civilization be fully self-explanatory. This means not only that it must begin at the beginning, with the origins of our civilization in ancient Israel and Greece, but that it must introduce every name or event that takes an integral place in the account and ruthlessly delete all others no matter how firmly imbedded in historical protocol. Only thus simplified and complete will the narrative present a sufficiently clear outline of those major trends and developments that have led from the beginning of our recorded time to the most pressing of our current problems. This simplification, however, need not involve intellectual dilution or evasion. On the contrary, it can effectively raise rather than lower the level of presentation. It is on this assumption that the present series has been based, and each contributor has been urged to write for a mature and literate audience. It is hoped, therefore, that the essays may also prove profitable and rewarding to readers outside the college classroom.

The plan of the first part of the series is to sketch, in related essays, the narrative of our history from its origins to the eve of the French Revolution; each is to be written by a recognized scholar and is designed to serve as the basic reading for one week in a semester course. The developments of the nineteenth and twentieth centuries will be covered in a succeeding series which will provide the same quantity of reading material for each week of the second semester. This scale of presentation has been adopted in the conviction that any understanding of the central problem of the preservation of the integrity and dignity of the individual human being depends first on an examination of the origins of our tradition in the politics and philosophy of the ancient Greeks and the religion of the ancient Hebrews and then on a relatively more detailed knowledge of its recent development within our industrial urban society.

The decision to devote equal space to twenty-five centuries and to a century and a half was based on analogy with the human memory. Those events most remote tend to be remembered in least detail but often with a sense of clarity and perspective that is absent in more recent and more crowded recollections. If the roots of our tradition must be identified, their relation to the present must be carefully developed. The nearer the narrative approaches contemporary times, the more difficult and complicated this becomes. Recent experience must be worked over more carefully and in more detail if it is to contribute effectively to an understanding of the contemporary world.

It may be objected that the series attempts too much. The attempt is being made, however, on the assumption that any historical development should be susceptible of meaningful treatment on any scale and in the realization that a very large proportion of today's college students do not have more time to invest in this part of their education. The practical alternative appears to lie between some attempt to create a new brief account of the history of our tradition and the abandonment of any serious effort to communicate the essence of that tradition to all but a handful of our students. It is the conviction of everyone contributing to this series that the second alternative must not be accepted by default.

In a series covering such a vast sweep of time, few scholars would find themselves thoroughly at home in the fields covered by more than one or two of the essays. This means, in practice, that almost every essay should be written by a different author. In spite of apparent drawbacks, this procedure promises real advantages. Each contributor will be in a position to set higher standards of accuracy and insight in an essay encompassing a major portion of the field of his life's work than could ordinarily be expected in surveys of some ten or twenty centuries. The inevitable discontinuity of style and interpretation could be modified by editorial coordination; but it was felt that some discontinuity was in itself desirable. No illusion is more easily acquired by the student in an elementary course, or is more prejudicial to the efficacy of such a course, than that a single smoothly articulated text represents the very substance of history itself. If the shift from author to author, week by week, raises difficulties for the beginning student, they are difficulties that will not so much impede his progress as contribute to his growth.

This essay, *Mediaeval Society* by Mr. Sidney Painter, offers an introduction to an understanding of everyday life in the early Middle Ages. Social history of this period has been studied intensively for years, but, in spite of this or perhaps in part because of it, few brief, concrete, and comprehensive accounts of daily existence in mediaeval Europe have appeared. To fill this gap, Mr. Painter was asked to write an essay that could be read at a sitting, that would outline the most important technical developments, and that would infuse this information with understanding and sympathy. He has succeeded in producing a swift summary equally fitted to enlighten the ignorance of the beginner or to illuminate the knowledge of the more advanced student.

The author and editor wish to express their gratitude to Mr. Joseph R. Strayer for many helpful suggestions.

EDWARD WHITING FOX

Ithaca, New York

Contents

MEDIAEVAL SOCIETY

Prolegomena〜〜〜〜〜〜〜〜〜〜〜〜

THE term Middle Ages was coined by European historians to describe the years between the collapse of Roman civilization and what seemed to them the dawn of their own era. As they were primarily interested in the history of northwestern Europe, England, France, and Germany, they chose their limiting dates accordingly. In general the Middle Ages were considered to extend from the deposition of Romulus Augustulus, the last Roman emperor to have his seat in the West, in 476 to about 1500. To these historians the period called the Renaissance was the beginning of the modern era. They placed its commencement in Italy in the fourteenth century and its spread over western Europe in the years just before and just after 1500. Thus in its original meaning Middle Ages described a period of about 1,000 years in northwestern Europe and about 850 years in Italy. But like most historical terms it has been used by different scholars to suit their own tastes. There has been a strong inclination to push the beginning of the period back to the death of Diocletian in 305. There has also been a feeling that it should include the same period in the history of eastern Europe. The great basic work on the history of the Middle Ages, the *Cambridge Mediaeval History*, begins with the death of Diocle-

tian and includes eastern Europe. Although the series of
which this essay forms a part contains a discussion of the
Byzantine empire, this essay itself restricts its range to western Europe and particularly to northwestern Europe. Thus
it is a description of mediaeval society in the narrow sense.

The environment in which the civilization that we call
mediaeval developed was far different from that of the
Roman Empire. The latter was essentially a Mediterranean
state and its people were preponderantly of the race that
anthropologists describe as Mediterranean. The lands that
rimmed the great inland sea had a mild, dry climate and in
general relatively infertile soils. Italy and Greece probably
had more fertile soils in classical times than they have today,
but it is doubtful that they were ever really rich. The only
parts of this region that were fertile by our standards were
the valley of the Nile and various irrigated districts in North
Africa. Roman agriculture was based on wheat and olives.
The light, dry soils were easy to work. The fame of the
cedars of Lebanon demonstrates the rarity of forests in the
Mediterranean lands.

Except in Italy, southern France, and the district around
Barcelona in Spain, mediaeval civilization in the sense in
which we are using the term did not touch the Mediterranean. And although these regions were important economically and culturally during the Middle Ages, they were
weak politically. The center of power in the mediaeval period lay far to the north in a very different environment. To
the north of the lowlands fringing the Mediterranean was a
region originally covered almost entirely by vast forests of
oak, ash, and beech. It was a well-watered country of mild
summers and cold winters with deep, heavy, fertile soils.
Here and there in the great forests the men of prehistoric

times had cleared land for their villages and fields. As time went on the settlements increased and more and more land was cleared, but the forests, though reduced in size, did not disappear. Moreover, the wet climate was suitable for rapid growth, and when a settlement was abandoned it soon became forest once again. In short, here was a land with great potentialities for agriculture but requiring far different techniques from those employed in the Mediterranean region.

Between the ninth and the fourth centuries before Christ this vast region stretching from the western shore of Ireland to the present frontiers of the Slavic peoples and from the North and Baltic seas to the Mediterranean was dominated by the Celts. In all probability the Celts were of the type called Alpine by anthropologists. Their political organization was essentially tribal, and they lived by farming and cattle raising. Soon after the fourth century B.C. the Celts began to feel the pressure from another expanding people— the Teutons or Germans. Starting from the Scandinavian peninsula the Germans slowly drove the Celts from the region now known as Germany. By the time Caesar invaded Gaul the Germans had occupied the country around the mouth of the Rhine and eastern England. Then for some four centuries their progress westward and southward was prevented by the armies of Rome. But when the Roman Empire began its collapse in the fourth and fifth centuries, the Germans began to move once more. They occupied northern Gaul, the valleys of the upper Rhône and Saône, the valley of the Po in northern Italy, and the part of Britain later called England. Although Germanic armed invaders ruled for considerable periods over central and southern Italy, southern France, Spain, and North Africa, their numbers were too small to affect the essential composition of the

population or the basic institutions of the regions. But by
the end of the sixth century A.D. northwestern Europe was a
German land. Only in Scotland, Wales, Ireland, and Brittany did a thin fringe of Celtic civilization survive.

The shift of the center of power in western Europe from
the Mediterranean region to the north and from Romans to
Germans is apparent when one glances at the situation in
A.D. 800. Charlemagne had been crowned in Rome as Roman emperor. He ruled Italy, Gaul, and a strip of northern
Spain and sought to have his imperial position recognized
by the Byzantine ruler in Constantinople. But Charlemagne
was essentially a German monarch ruling a German state.
The center of his power lay in the regions on both banks of
the lower Rhine, and his favorite residence was Aachen.
Even his power in Italy rested on the possession of a German crown and the rule over a German people, the Lom-
bards. Outside of Charlemagne's empire were two important
groups of Germanic peoples: the Anglo-Saxons in England
and the Scandinavian inhabitants of Denmark, Norway, and
Sweden. Beyond to the west lay the remnants of Celtic civilization. Scots from Ireland had conquered the Picts and established the kingdom of Scotland. South of the Clyde river
in southwest Scotland and northwest England lay the Celtic
kingdom of Strathclyde. Various Celtic chiefs and princes
ruled Wales and Ireland. Brittany was held by Celts who
had fled from Britain before the advancing Anglo-Saxons.

To the south of Charlemagne's realm lay the lands of the
Moslem empire. Except for the march of Barcelona conquered by Charlemagne, Spain was held by the Moslems.
They also ruled North Africa and were pressing naval attacks against the islands of the western Mediterranean and
even the coasts of southern Gaul. To the east from the Bal-

tic to the Danube the Carolingian empire touched the lands
of the Slavs. Although Charlemagne conducted a number of
military expeditions beyond the Elbe and the Saale rivers
that formed the eastern border of the German lands, they
were chiefly punitive in nature, and he made no attempt to
hold the country. The reconquest of eastern Germany was
left for the mediaeval German kings and their vassals. South
of the Danube the sons of Charlemagne in command of his
Lombard cavalry drove the Avars, close relatives of the
Huns, out of the lands at the head of the Adriatic Sea. Finally, the east coast of Italy and Sicily still recognized the
rule of the Byzantine emperor.

The ninth century saw the Christian states of western
Europe, the Carolingian empire, Anglo-Saxon England, and
the Celtic lands, all victims of new non-Christian invaders.
From Scandinavia was launched the last great wave of Germanic migrations. Two forces seem to have been behind this
movement: overpopulation and the development of the
Scandinavian monarchies. The former made it hard to find
a living at home and hence encouraged men to seek their
fortunes abroad, while the growth of royal power meant
better internal order and hence less attractive conditions for
lovers of war and rapine. In the ninth century the people of
Scandinavia were divided into two groups—farmers who
tilled the soil and Vikings who fought. It was the Vikings
who first took to their ships and began to ravage the western
coasts of Europe. At first it was simply a matter of summer
plundering expeditions, but soon the Vikings were winter-
ing in other lands and extending their raids inland. The Low
Countries, western France, and the British Isles were thoroughly ravaged. Where they found favorable conditions,
the Vikings would take possession of a region. In such cases

they were soon followed by migrant farmers from their homeland looking for new lands to cultivate. Charles the Simple, king of the West Franks, gave a Viking chief the lands about the mouth of the Seine in the hope that he would protect the realm from other Vikings. Although Charles's new subjects were able to keep the plunderers at bay, they sought more land for themselves until they occupied all of what was later called Normandy—the land of the Northmen. In England the Vikings fought a long, fierce war with Alfred, king of Wessex and chief king of England, which resulted at last in a treaty dividing the country between them. The sons and grandsons of Alfred reconquered the Danish region, but it retained a heavy Scandinavian population. The Vikings also took possession of the Celtic kingdom of Strathclyde and extended it to cover what is now Lancashire. Other Vikings occupied the islands off the west coast of Scotland and the Isle of Man in the Irish Sea. In the thirteenth century there was still a Scandinavian king of the Isles with his seat on Man. The Vikings also invaded Ireland and for a time ruled a large part of it. The chief Irish towns, Dublin, Waterford, and Wexford, were originally Viking strongholds. Finally Vikings and farmers settled Iceland, went on to Greenland, and apparently for a time maintained a settlement on the coast of North America.

The Viking raiders along the coasts of the North Sea and the Atlantic Ocean were Danes and Norwegians. The Swedes turned to the east. They occupied almost the entire shore of the Baltic Sea and pressed on into the Slavic lands. They established strongholds such as Novgorod and Kiev and from them ruled the native Slavs. By the end of the ninth century a series of Viking principalities extended from Novgorod to the Black Sea. These states were in commercial contact with Constantinople, were eventually converted to Christianity by Byzantine missionaries, and so became part of the civilization of eastern Europe.

While the Vikings were harassing the north of Christian Europe, the Moslem power was spreading in the south. During the ninth century they seized the Balearic Islands, Sicily, Sardinia, and Corsica, invaded southern Italy, and even laid siege to Rome. By 900 they were almost absolute masters of the western Mediterranean. Meanwhile the eastern part of the Carolingian empire had still another foe: the Magyars, a Mongolian people closely related to the Huns and Avars. The Magyars occupied the great Hungarian plain and conducted continual raids into eastern Germany.

The attacks on Christian Europe by its foes came to an end in the tenth and eleventh centuries. The grant of Normandy to Rollo in 911 practically ended the Viking raids on France. By 939 the grandson of Alfred had reconquered the part of England occupied by the Danes. But in England the victory was temporary. Late in the tenth century the Danes came again, not as raiders but as a well-organized army under Swein, king of Denmark, and Swein and his son Canute ruled England for over twenty years. In fact, England did not become safe from the Danes until William, duke of Normandy, conquered the country and established an effective military system supported by a vast network of fortresses. The Magyar invasions of Germany were stopped in 955 by Otto I's great victory at the Lechfeld. Fierce adventurers from Normandy drove the Moslems from southern Italy and Sicily during the years 1057–1091 and established the Norman kingdom of Naples and Sicily. The eleventh century also saw the Moslems ejected from Corsica and Sardinia by the fleets of Genoa and Pisa.

The end of the period of invasions saw western Europe in a sad state. There were no towns in the economic sense, and the clusters of buildings around cathedrals and abbeys lay in ruins. The population had greatly decreased, and a great deal of land once cultivated had become forest or at least brush. Although we have no figures and any statement on the subject is a pure guess, it seems likely that the population of France about 950 was smaller than it had been at any time since the Roman conquest. For England we have a reasonably reliable estimate for the year 1086 of 1,100,000. In all probability this too represents the lowest point reached by the population of England since the Saxon settlement. But with the end of the invasions society began to recover and to form the institutions described in this essay. While the roots of mediaeval civilization lay deep in the past, it grew and flowered during the eleventh, twelfth, and thirteenth centuries. The time schedule was different in different lands. The feudal system started in France and spread to England, Italy, Germany, and Palestine. Feudal institutions also played an important part in Christian Spain and Scandinavia. The seignorial system seems to have developed simultaneously in England, France, and western Germany, and it too spread in various forms over most of Europe. Obviously no single essay can describe the many forms taken by these institutions in different countries. Mediaeval society as it will appear in this essay was that of France, England, and western Germany.

One might say that nothing but the arbitrary arrogance of English, French, and German historians can account for the selection of so small a part of Europe to discuss in detail under the heading mediaeval society. To some extent this is, of course, true. A Russian historian would obviously devote more attention to eastern Europe. But the selection of this region cannot be called purely arbitrary. This essay is intended for students in the United States, and the origins of our institutions lie in those of western Europe. Moreover, as has been suggested in the previous paragraph, many of the institutions that eventually spread over Europe as a whole originated in this region. The seignorial system was carried into the regions reconquered by the Germans from the Slavs, spread to the neighboring Slavs and eventually to Russia. Furthermore, every Russian historian today is deeply affected by the development of civilization in western Europe. The theory of history enunciated by Karl Marx was based on the history of the western nations, and Soviet historians can ignore this theory only at their peril.

Finally, although this region was a small part of the total area of Europe, its climate, soil, topography, racial structure, and culture gave it a unity that would be hard to find in any other major segment of the continent. From the border of Wales to the river Elbe and from the North and Baltic seas to the mountains of Auvergne and the Alps the country as a whole was reasonably fertile and well watered. There were hilly sections, but except for the Harz country in Saxony there were no mountains. Between the villages were forests, and land left untilled soon returned to that state. The climate was mild in summer and cold in winter; the soils were deep and heavy. In short, throughout this region the same agricultural technique was effective. The racial structure was also much the same everywhere. Prehistoric peoples had been conquered by Celts and Celts in turn by Germans. The proportions of Nordic and Alpine stock in the population might differ from district to district, yet the basic ingredients were the same. Then too these peoples were bound together by the Roman Christian culture and the Roman Catholic faith. Although the spoken tongues varied widely, throughout the entire region Latin was the language of reading and writing. A clerk in the court of the English king could easily understand the decrees of a German emperor, and both could study the political system of Rome in the *Institutes* of Justinian. Again, from district to district church practice differed somewhat and different local saints were venerated, but the dominant beliefs were the same and all people looked for spiritual guidance to St. Peter's successors in Rome. Thus the peoples of England, France, and Germany had a common heritage and common problems.

CHAPTER I

The Feudal System and the Feudal Caste

DURING the period that is known as the Middle Ages the basic centers of political, economic, and social life were the castle, the village, and the town. The people who lived in each of these had their own peculiar institutions. Continental historians as a rule use the term "feudal system" to describe the dominant institutions of the castle and the village, but English and American writers are inclined to restrict this term to the institutions that flourished among the noble castle dwellers and to call those of the inhabitants of the village the seignorial or manorial system. In this book "feudal system" will be used in the narrow sense to describe the institutions of the noble class while "seignorial system" will designate those of the villagers.

The fundamental elements of the feudal system were the lord, the vassal, and the fief. The vassal entered into an intimate subordinate personal relationship with the lord by swearing fidelity and doing homage to him. He might or might not receive from the lord a fief—that is, the use of something of value, usually a piece of land with its peasant inhabitants. It seems possible that the oath of fidelity established a purely personal relationship without any economic considerations, while homage implied the furnishing of food and clothing even when no fief was granted, but this distinction cannot be conclusively established. Many scholars have attempted to draw a clear distinction between fidelity and homage, but their efforts have not been successful. In general all vassals swore fidelity and did homage. When a vassal was given a fief, he was expected to perform certain services in return for it. The inauguration of the relationship between a lord and a vassal was a solemn ceremony. The vassal knelt before the lord, placed his two hands between the lord's hands, and swore fidelity to him. If a fief was being granted, the lord usually gave the vassal some symbol, such as a clod of earth. As these arrangements between lords and vassals formed the basic political structure for much of western Europe during the Middle Ages and have profoundly influenced our own political institutions, they deserve extended consideration.

The Origins of Feudalism

The origins of feudal institutions may be found in both Roman and German life. According to Tacitus, when a German war chief planned a campaign, he gathered about him a group of picked warriors which was called his *comitatus*. These men swore absolute fidelity and obedience to the chief in return for arms, food, clothing, and a share in the plunder. The German chieftains who set themselves up as kings in the Roman Empire had similar bands of sworn followers. The Frankish kings called the *comitatus* a *truste* and its members *antrustiones*. The Saxon kings were surrounded by bands of *thanes*. Thus the practice of a warrior binding himself by an oath to follow a chief in war was well established among the Germanic peoples. The Romans had a somewhat similar institution, the *clientela*. When a Roman freed a slave, the freedman usually remained a dependent of his former master, a *cliens*. Poor freemen might seek the protection of a senator by becoming his clients. In the latter years of the Roman Empire in the West the *comitatus* and the clientele tended to become merged into one institution. The great Roman nobles hired bands of German warriors to serve as their bodyguards. These warriors were known as *bucellarii*. Now the Roman senator may well have thought of his *bucellarii* as soldier-clients, but the Germans were more likely to consider themselves members of a *comitatus*. The *bucellarii* played an extremely important part in the wars of the fifth century: a large part of Belisarius' army was composed of his *bucellarii*. It seems clear that we have in these various Roman, German, and Romano-German institutions the prototype of the relationship between lord and vassal.

There is no evidence that the early Germans knew any form of land tenure other than simple ownership, but the Romans had a number of forms of dependent tenures. There was the *precarium*, a grant of land in return for some form of rent that could be terminated whenever the grantor saw fit. Then there was the *beneficium* that was usually given for a fixed term, sometimes for life. These tenures were taken over by the Germans who settled in the Empire. In Merovingian Gaul the church used the *beneficium* very freely to obtain men to cultivate its lands. Thus the conception of dependent tenures held by men who were personally free was well known to the Romano-German world.

Charles Martel

When Charles Martel became duke of the Franks, he had great need of a strong and reliable military force. Only a body of soldiers whom he could trust could secure his dominance over the turbulent Frankish nobles, who had gotten completely out of hand since his father's death. Then the Frankish state faced for the first time in its history dangerous external foes. The Saxons were pressing against the eastern frontier while to the south the Moslems had conquered the Visigothic kingdom of Spain and were crossing the Pyrenees. Now the most effective type of soldier known to Charles was a mounted warrior armed with sword and lance and protected by a shield, helmet, and body armor. But horses, arms, and armor were so expensive that only a few Frankish nobles could afford them. Moreover, their efficient use in war required training and continuous practice. They would be useless to a man who had to wrest his living from the cultivation of his land. The Byzantine emperor could hire soldiers and equip them, but in western Europe by the eighth century the general economic system had decayed so far that Charles had little or no money revenue. The only way to support the soldiers he needed was to give them land and the labor to work the land. Charles arrived at a very simple solution. The Frankish church possessed vast tracts of land cultivated by its tenants. Charles compelled the church to give extensive *beneficia* or benefices to his soldiers. These soldiers took an oath of fidelity to Charles and promised to serve him as long as they lived.

The Vassi Dominici

Charles called these soldiers *vassi dominici* or vassals of the lord. The term *vassus* or vassal was an old one in Merovingian Gaul, but before Charles's time it seems to have usually meant a person of very lowly station. Charles's *vassi* served him well against the Frankish nobles, the Moslems,

and the Saxons. His descendants steadily incre
number. Both Pepin and Charlemagne were acc
give benefices in conquered lands to *vassi do*
would thus form a sort of permanent garrison.

With the Carolingian *vassi dominici* and their benefices
we have all the fundamental elements of the feudal system.
The *vassus* swears fidelity to his lord, receives a benefice to
support him, and performs military service for the lord. In
short, feudal institutions existed in the Carolingian state, but
they lacked many of the features of later feudalism and they
were far from universal. The benefices of the *vassi dominici*
occupied only a small part of the Frankish state, and most
Frankish nobles and freemen held their lands in full ownership. Lands held in this way were usually known as alods to
distinguish them from benefices.

During the years between the death of Charlemagne in
814 and the accession of Hugh Capet in 987 feudalism spread
over the West Frankish state until it embraced almost all
the land and its free inhabitants. Unfortunately the historical sources for this period are extremely scanty and hence
little is known of the process by which feudalism developed.
One can, however, make fairly satisfactory hypotheses. This
century and a half was a time of almost continual turmoil.
Fierce Vikings raided the coasts of France, sailed up its
rivers, and even conducted expeditions across country. The
wild Magyar riders from the plains of Hungary harried the
eastern part of the land. Moslem plunderers occupied the
delta of the Rhône and ravaged the neighboring region.
Moreover, the country was torn by civil wars. First there
were bitter rivalries between various members of the Carolingian royal house and later a long struggle between the
Carolingians and the Capetians. In short, during these years

there was rarely a government capable of keeping order and defending the realm from outside enemies. Great land-owners obtained soldiers by giving benefices to able war-riors. Small landowners sought the protection of greater men by becoming their vassals. They would give up their alodial holding to a lord and receive it back as a fief. The royal *vassi dominici*, finding the king unable to protect them, became the vassals of local dignitaries. Once in a while the sources reveal a glimpse of what was happening. An early biography of St. Leger, bishop of Auxerre, explains that be-fore he entered the church he was a royal *vassus dominicus*. He vigorously resisted the demands of the local count that he give up his direct relationship to the king and become his vassal. But clearly most *vassi* had to give way before the power of the local magnate.

The Feudal Hierarchy

Although the process is obscure, the result is quite clear. By 987 the soldiers of the West Frankish state were arranged in a feudal hierarchy bound together by oaths of vassalage. The king was at the top of the feudal pyramid: the suzerain of the land. A few dukes and counts were his direct vassals. They in turn had their vassals, rear vassals, and rear rear vas-sals. At the bottom of the pyramid was the simple knight with just enough land and peasant labor to support him, his family, and his horses. Now this structure was not all em-bracing by 987; in fact, it never was. As late as the latter part of the twelfth century the count of Dreux surrendered large alodial holdings to the count of Champagne and received them back as fiefs. A recent study has shown that large alo-dial estates persisted throughout the Middle Ages in the re-gion around Bordeaux. But in comparison with the total area of the country these exceptions were of slight importance, and the principle beloved by feudal lawyers—no land without a lord—became essentially true. Thus all land was someone's fief and every landholder except the king was someone's vassal. The soldiers, the knights, held the land of France, and they were bound together by the feudal system.

The development and definition of the rights and obligations of lords and vassals was a long, slow process that extended over five centuries, from the eighth to the thirteenth. At the beginning the vassal can have had few if any rights against his lord; the benefice was often revocable at the lord's will and was never hereditary. But in practice only a strong king can have been able to prevent a vigorous warrior from succeeding to his father's benefice. This is evident as early as the reign of Charles the Bald. When Charles was about to leave for Rome to assume the imperial crown, he decreed that if the holder of a royal benefice should die during his absence, the vassal's son should hold the benefice until his return to France. It is clear that by the end of the ninth century the benefice had become hereditary. This gave the vassal and his family proprietary rights in the benefice or fief. It also made it necessary to define the mutual obligations of lord and vassal. Obviously this would come about through an endless series of disputes over particular questions, between individual lords and vassals. Perhaps the most important single feature of the feudal system was its method of settling such disputes. When a lord and his vassal disagreed, the question was settled by all the vassals of the lord. The lord presided over the assembly, called his *curia* or court, but the vassals made the decision. Thus in each fief there developed a body of custom governing the relation between the lord and his vassals. Although historians often speak of "feudal law," there was in reality no such thing—each feudal court had its own law. Hence when we describe feudal customs we are making generalizations based on many different sets of laws. The following account of the rights and obligations of lords and vassals would probably not be exactly correct for any particular fief.

Military Service

As the fundamental purpose of the feudal system was effective military organization, the basic obligation of a vassal to his lord was military service. In the beginning there is little doubt that the vassal was expected to serve his lord as a soldier as frequently and for as long periods as the lord desired. But as time went on the vassals began to distinguish between different types of military service and to limit their obligations in regard to some of them. When the lord's fief was being invaded by an enemy, the vassals were clearly bound to aid him until the danger was over. Offensive action by the lord against a neighbor was a different matter. By the twelfth century at least the vassals of most fiefs had limited their obligation in a war of this sort. Perhaps the most common rule was that the vassal should serve the lord for forty days. In some fiefs the arrangement was that he was obliged to serve forty days at his own cost and another forty days if the lord offered to feed him.

A simple knight holding just enough land to support himself and his family, what feudal lawyers called a knight's fief or knight's fee, could only serve his lord with his own right arm. But what of the powerful vassal who had enfeoffed many knights; could he fulfill his obligation to his lord by simply offering his personal service? Here it is almost impossible to make any useful generalization. It depended largely on the respective power of lord and vassals. The petty vassals of the count of Champagne owed him the service of a number of knights roughly proportionate to the size of their fiefs, but the greater vassals like the count of Grandpré owed only their personal service in the count's army. In Normandy every fief owed a set quota of knights to the duke's host, and William the Conqueror established this system in England. As the Norman dukes were strong lords, their vassals owed them a good proportion of their available knights —581 out of 1,500. But the great lords of France, the direct vassals of the French crown, owed the Capetian king ridiculously small contingents. The count of Champagne who had some 2,039 knightly vassals owed but 10 to the royal army. In general one can say that the vassal was inclined to argue that his personal service fulfilled his obligation no matter how large his fief might be, but that he could rarely succeed in maintaining this position. Usually he was obliged to lead to his lord's army some proportion of his own knightly vassals.

In addition to serving as knights in their army most lords expected their vassals to provide garrisons for their fortresses. During the tenth century the castle became an important element in the feudal military system of France. The earliest castles were artificial mounds of earth surrounded by a ditch or moat. On top of the mound was a palisade of wood. Often a wooden tower stood inside the palisade. The more pretentious fortresses would have one or even two areas enclosed by moat and palisade. In the terminology of the day the mound and its fortifications were called the motte and the adjacent fortified areas baileys. By the eleventh century very powerful lords were building stone towers—massive structures with walls twenty to thirty feet thick. These were called "towers" and were usually surrounded by moats. Thus there were two types of castle: the motte and bailey and the tower. By the twelfth century some stonework was being added to motte and bailey castles. Usually the first part to be reinforced was the gate—a stone-gate tower could not be easily burned. Later large rectangular stone buildings called keeps replaced the motte as the central stronghold of the castle. Still later, stone walls replaced the wooden palisades, and by the thirteenth century these stone walls were usually reinforced by towers.

Most lords of any importance had household knights, men they armed, fed, and clothed, who safeguarded the castle in which they resided in time of peace. But in case of war a more adequate garrison was required. Then many lords had several castles and had to provide garrisons for all of them. The vassals performed this duty of castle-guard under a wide variety of arrangements. A petty lord with only one castle might require certain of his knights to garrison it in time of war. A lord with several castles might divide his knights into groups with each group being responsible for one of his castles. Thus the lands of the count of Champagne were divided into *castellanies*. The knights holding fiefs in a castellany were obliged to perform castle-guard duty in its castle. In England the king provided for the garrisoning of his castles by demanding knights for guard duty from his vassals. Nine fiefs provided a permanent garrison of twenty-two knights for the great royal fortress of Dover. In general one can say that most knights owed guard duty at a castle. Sometimes it was only in case of war, but often it was an annual period of service. The knights of the great barony of Richmond in England owed three months' annual service in Richmond castle.

Court Service

Next in importance to military service was what is usually known as court service. In some fiefs the lord could summon his vassals to his court whenever he pleased. In others their attendance was confined to certain fixed times of year. These assemblies of vassals had several purposes. We have already seen that disputes between lord and vassal over the services due from the vassal's fief were settled by all the lord's vassals in his court. If a vassal committed any offense against his lord, it was tried in this court. Moreover, disputes between vassals of the same lord came to the lord's tribunal. This was the well-known trial by equals or peers that played so important a part in feudal custom. A lord could not legally attack a vassal or deprive him of his fief without a judgment of his peers. Actually in early feudal custom the judgment by the peers meant simply that a reasonable case had been made against the accused, but only if he refused to appear to answer the charge was it a condemnation. If the accused appeared and denied his guilt, one of the vassals who had rendered the judgment had to prove him guilty by defeating him in battle. Thus service in the feudal court could be both onerous and dangerous.

Another purpose of these solemn assemblies of vassals was to give their lord advice. The efficient conduct of the business of the fief was a subject of mutual interest to both lord and vassals, and the former was expected to seek the latter's counsel before taking any important decision. Thus the marriage of the lord was a matter of grave concern to his vassals. A well-chosen wife might add greatly to the lord's power and the strength of the fief as a whole, while a poorly chosen one might be disastrous. Suppose a lord was wavering between two ladies, each of whom would bring a strong castle as a marriage portion. The vassals would want to weigh carefully the strategic value of the two fortresses before advising their lord as to which girl he should marry. A wise lord also asked his vassals' advice before starting a war or any other venture in which he needed their aid. Finally, changes in the custom of the fief were made by the lord with the approval of his vassals. When the kings of England issued decrees, they were careful to record that it was done with the advice and assent of their vassals.

Then at times a lord might want his vassals around him for a quite different purpose. A nobleman's prestige depended on his military power, and military power consisted largely of knightly vassals who would follow him to war. Hence when a lord wanted to make a show of his importance, he summoned his vassals to court. Perhaps it was for the wedding of his daughter or the knighting of his son. Perhaps the king or a great duke was coming on a visit. But whatever the occasion, the vassals were expected to appear to "do honor to their lord." When the writers of romances wanted to indicate how mighty some nobleman was, they described the number and importance of the vassals who surrounded him.

Although military and court service were the personal obligations common to all vassals, in particular cases the feudal agreement might call for the performance of other duties. The seneschal who was the chief administrative officer of the household and the fief, the constable who commanded the lord's castle, the marshal who supervised the care of the war horses, the butler who saw to the wine supply, and any other officials the lord might need who were of knightly rank received fiefs in return for their services. In the barony of Richmond the lord's two chief vassals were the seneschal and the constable. The most powerful vassal of the earl of Chester was the constable of Chester.

Economic Obligations

In addition to personal services a vassal had certain economic obligations to his lord. One of these was a payment called relief. The origin of relief can probably be found in offers made by a vassal or his son to secure the renewal of the agreement under which a benefice was held when it was terminated by the death of either the lord or the vassal. Thus when a lord died, his vassals would offer his heir some inducement to grant them the benefices they held from his predecessor. The son of a vassal would also offer the lord something in return for receiving his father's benefice. When fiefs became hereditary, these customary payments remained. The relief due at the death of the lord soon disappeared; only occasional cases of it can be found in the eleventh century. But the relief due from the vassal's heir when he inherited the fief became a regular feudal obligation. In the tenth and eleventh centuries before money was readily obtainable relief was usually a payment in goods; the horse and armor of the deceased vassal was the most common requirement. Later it became a money payment. The amount varied with the relative bargaining powers of lord and vassal, but there seems to have been a general feeling that it should represent a year's income from the fief.

A vassal was expected to come to his lord's aid whenever he needed assistance. If the lord was captured in war, it was the duty of his vassals to contribute to the payment of his ransom. When the prestige of the lord required that he put on a particularly magnificent celebration, the vassals were expected to bear part of the expense. If the lord planned a crusade or a long and costly pilgrimage, he might ask his vassals to help him. In short, whenever a lord saw himself faced with unusual expenses, he was inclined to ask his vassals for an "aid." Obviously under an impecunious and extravagant lord this obligation could become a serious burden on the vassals. As time went on a distinction was drawn between the occasions when the lord could demand an aid as a right and those on which he had to rely on the good will of his vassals. All lords had the right to demand an aid on three occasions: when the lord was a prisoner and had to be ransomed, when he married his eldest daughter, and when he made his eldest son a knight. In some fiefs the vassals were obliged to contribute when the lord paid relief for his fief. If the lord wanted an aid for any other purpose, he had to persuade his vassals to give it to him.

Feudal Privileges

Besides being entitled to the services owed by his vassal, the lord had certain privileges that grew out of the nature of the feudal contract. A vassal could not give his daughter in marriage without his lord's consent. When a girl was married, she carried with her as a marriage portion a part of her father's fief. As this meant that her husband would control land held from the lord, he had the right to make certain that the husband was not one who was likely to be his foe. Then when a vassal died leaving a daughter as heiress or a son who was a minor, the lord had the right to insist that some adult male should perform the service due from the fief. If the daughter was of marriageable age, the lord could select a husband for her—in fact it was his duty to do so. In the case of a minor heir or heiress some adult male had to be given custody of the fief. Here feudal custom varied greatly. A very common rule was to give the custody to the nearest male relative on the mother's side, usually her eldest brother. As he could never succeed to the fief, he was not tempted to do away with the young heir. An uncle on the father's side was a less reliable guardian since he would inherit if the heir were to die. But in many regions the right of custody belonged to the lord. This was true in Normandy, in England, and in other important feudal states. The lord would appoint someone as his representative to look after the fief and perform the service due from it.

Under certain circumstances a lord could seize a fief that was held of him. If a vassal failed to perform the services due from his fief or committed any serious offense against his lord, his peers assembled in the lord's court could condemn him to forfeit his fief. Then if a vassal died without heirs, his fief passed to the lord by escheat. Obviously the frequency of escheat would depend on the rules of inheritance. In theory all descendants of a holder of the fief were possible heirs to it, but in most regions this right of inheritance was restricted in practice. The rights of the brothers, sisters, uncles, and aunts of the last tenant were almost universally recognized. First cousins were commonly accepted as heirs. But unless a second cousin was a powerful man whose friendship the lord needed, his chances were usually very slight.

The Operation of the Feudal System

Having described the origins, development, and general nature of feudalism, it seems worth while to make some comments on how the system actually operated. One obvious question is: At what stage in the feudal hierarchy from king to simple knight did the most effective power rest? In the tenth and eleventh centuries before the reappearance of a money economy it seems clear that the most powerful link in the feudal chain was the lowest vassal who possessed a strong castle. If a simple knight who did not have a castle defied his lord and the judgment of his peers given in the lord's court, he could be disciplined with comparative ease. But a strong castle adequately garrisoned made a man almost immune from punishment. It was a poor castle indeed that, given a determined garrison with sufficient supplies, could not hold out for forty days, and few feudal armies could be held together longer than that. If a great feudal prince like the duke of Normandy or the count of Champagne was determined to crush some vassal who had a strong castle, he could do it by calling up part of his feudal levy at a time and so maintaining the siege until the castle was taken, but rarely did anyone want to discipline a vassal that badly. In short, the baron, the man who had one or two strong castles and whose vassals were simple knights, was relatively the most powerful figure in the feudal hierarchy. He could effectively discipline his own vassals and could defy his lord with impunity.

It is important to remember that the feudal system was devised by the warrior class of France to furnish the necessary minimum of political and military co-operation while imposing the least possible restraint on the individual knight. It was the blackest of crimes—a felony—for a vassal to strike his lord, seduce his wife or daughter, or commit any personal offense against his lord. If he murdered a fellow vassal or raped his wife, he could be called to answer for the offense in the lord's court. But as far as feudal custom was concerned he could murder with complete impunity the vassal of some lord other than his own. And feudal law had no interest whatever in his behavior toward anyone not a member of the feudal class. In tenth- and eleventh-century France where the feudal system was almost the only effective political force, the members of the feudal class had almost complete personal freedom. As the basic function of this class was fighting, it was bound to be an age of turbulence and violence.

As a matter of fact, even where the feudal system should in theory have checked the warlike tendencies of the nobles, it did not do so very effectively. Although two vassals of the same lord could settle their disputes in his court, they usually preferred to wage war on each other, and the lord was inclined to let them fight it out. Disputes between a lord and his vassal often if not usually led to war. Only a weak and low-spirited vassal would accept an unfavorable decision by his lord's court; in a matter of any moment, it had to be enforced by arms. Then if a vassal felt that his lord had treated him unjustly, he could issue a formal defiance, renounce his oath of homage, and go to war against the lord. If he was defeated, he might lose his fief, but he could usually rely on the assistance of some enemy of his lord, and after a pleasant little war the affair would be amiably compromised.

Knighthood

The life of the male members of the feudal class was almost entirely devoted to preparing for and pursuing their occupation: fighting. In the belief that parents, in particular the mother, would be too indulgent toward a boy, the young noble was sent off when he was seven or eight to be brought up in another feudal household, usually that of his parent's lord or some close relative. Thus young William Marshal was placed in the care of a relative, the chamberlain of Tancarville. The boy was then taught to care for arms, armor, and war horses and to handle them in practice. He lived the hard, rough life best calculated to prepare him for a career as a warrior. When he was considered ready to take his place in battle, usually when he was about twenty or twenty-one, he was given his arms in a solemn ceremony. He knelt before an experienced knight and received a stroke by the hand or the flat of the sword. In the early days this seems to have been a terrific blow intended to knock him out if possible. Later it became a gentle ceremonial tap on the shoulder. This was the "dubbing" of a knight. Once the young man had received his arms and the blow, he was a full-fledged knight. A king could not rule nor could an heir take over the conduct of his fief until he was made a knight. It was the mark of coming of age.

The knight passed most of his time fighting, practicing with his arms, and hunting. Hunting meant riding, violent exercise, and often a dangerous battle with some formidable animal like a wild boar. It was thus closely akin to fighting. When in the twelfth century the growing power of the feudal princes and their desire to keep some sort of order in their lands began to reduce the amount of feudal warfare, the nobles held mock battles called tournaments. A great lord who felt that life was too dull and peaceful would send word around the countryside that he would hold a tournament on a certain day. The knights who came would be divided into two parties and would fight a regular pitched battle. The only differences between these early tournaments and real battles were that refuges were provided where knights could arm themselves and the injured seek safety and that those who were captured were not actually put in prison. But knights captured in a tournament were expected to pay ransom just as if they had been taken in war. These early tournaments were just about as dangerous as actual battle. It is, however, important to remember that feudal warfare was not very lethal. The knights were well protected by armor, and no one as a rule had any desire to kill his foe. A dead enemy was just a useless corpse, and the slain man's son was ready to take his place as your foe. But a captive could be held for ransom: a large sum of money or perhaps a village or a strong castle. The decisive battle of Lincoln in 1217 where some five hundred knights fought on each side resulted in the death of one man of knightly rank, and everyone felt very badly about the unfortunate occurrence.

The Place of Women

The women of the feudal caste spent most of their time in spinning, weaving, sewing, and general supervision of the household. Their status was a peculiar one. Under early feudal custom a woman was always in the custody of some male: first her father, then her husband. A widow was in the custody of her lord or her eldest son. A woman could inherit a fief, but she could rule it only through her husband. The reason for this is perfectly obvious. The function of the feudal class was to fight and a woman could not do that. She had no rights whatever against her husband. The writers of the romances clearly consider it quite in order for a husband to knock his wife down and stamp on her face because she annoyed him. The church tried to protect the wife to some extent by limiting the size of the stick with which her husband could beat her, but it also emphasized the fact that she was the chief source of the world's sin. Never-theless, though the feudal wife was a very inferior partner, she was her husband's partner. She had no rights he was bound to respect, but she was after him the mistress of his castle and his fief. In the lord's absence vassals, officials, and servants obeyed the lord's wife. In short, although she was without rights toward her husband, she shared his status toward all others.

The Standard of Living

On the material side the life of the feudal class was rough and uncomfortable. The castles were cold and drafty. If a castle was of wood, you had no fire, and if a stone castle allowed you to have one, you smothered in the smoke. Until the thirteenth century no one except a few great feudal princes had a castle providing more than two rooms. In the hall the lord did his business: received his officials and vas-sals, held his court, and entertained ordinary guests. There the family and retainers ate on trestle tables that at night served as beds for the servants and guests. The chamber was the private abode of the lord and his family. The lord and lady slept in a great bed, their children had smaller beds, and their personal servants slept on the floor. Distinguished visitors were entertained in the chamber. When the lord of the castle wanted a private talk with a guest, they sat on the bed. The lord and his family could have all the food they could eat, but it was limited in variety. Great platters of game, both birds and beasts, were the chief stand-by, rein-forced with bread and vast quantities of wine. They also had plenty of clothing, but the quality was largely limited by the capacity of the servant girls who made it. In short, in the tenth and eleventh centuries the noble had two resources, land and labor. But the labor was magnificently in-efficient and by our standards the land was badly tilled. Not until the revival of trade could the feudal class begin to live in anything approaching luxury.

Religious Faith

In accord with the atmosphere of the age in which they lived the members of the feudal aristocracy were intensely devout. With some few possible exceptions they accepted absolutely the teachings of the Christian church. They might sin with vigor and enthusiasm, but they repented and atoned equally thoroughly. Although the crusaders who set forth to fight the Moslems in Spain and the Holy Land were by no means moved by purely spiritual considerations, there can be little doubt that their paramount motive was the de-sire for salvation. Moreover, every fief of any importance had its monastic establishment, and the great feudal families were the founders and patrons of numerous monasteries. Every lord had his chaplain and every feudal residence some sort of a chapel. A large proportion of the gross revenues of most fiefs were assigned to religious purposes, and by the thirteenth century we find once important baronies reduced to insignificance by generations of munificent friends of the church. One must, moreover, be careful not to judge the devoutness of a feudal lord by individual acts. Peter of Dreux, duke of Brittany, was a bitter foe of the Breton bishops and was guilty of atrocities against certain clergy-men. At times his actions seemed those of a complete sceptic. Yet he built the south porch of Chartres cathedral and went on two crusades, in addition to making many gifts to cathe-dral chapters and monastic houses.

Chivalry

During the eleventh and twelfth centuries there grew out of the environment and way of life of the feudal class a system of ethical ideas that we call chivalry: virtues appropriate to the knight or chevalier. Chivalry was not a logical, consistent system of ethics. Its basic ideas sprang from a variety of sources and were often inconsistent with one another. Hence it is convenient to speak of three types of chivalry. In what may be called "feudal chivalry" the basic ideas developed naturally out of the way of life of the feudal noble. "Religious chivalry," on the other hand, represented the church's conception of the ideal knight. Finally, the ideas that are usually called those of "courtly love" were nourished by the ladies and by men whose chief object was to please them.

The German warriors had brought with them into the Roman Empire an admiration for the warrior virtues: courage and prowess in battle. They also valued the sound judgment that the feudal age was to call wisdom and fidelity to one's plighted word, later known as loyalty. Respect for these virtues was not a recent acquisition of the Frankish nobles. Their importance among the Germanic peoples can be clearly seen by a reader of the Norse sagas and Anglo-Saxon literature. But they were peculiarly applicable to feudal society. A man whose chief function was fighting had to be brave and effective in battle. Wisdom was a necessary attribute of the successful captain. The whole structure of the feudal system depended on respect for one's oath of homage and fidelity. These were the basic feudal virtues and formed the core of feudal chivalry.

The earliest ethical ideas of the feudal class concerned

their chief occupation and were designed to make war more pleasant for its participants. Armor was heavy and extremely hot under the blazing sun. No knight wanted to wear his armor when he was simply riding about, yet no knight was ever entirely safe from sudden attack by an enemy. Hence the idea developed that it was highly improper to attack an unarmed knight. You could ambush your foe, but you did not attack him until he had had time to put on his armor and prepare for battle. Then the chief purpose of feudal warfare was to take prisoners who could be ransomed. In the early days you put your prisoner in chains and dumped him in an unused storage bin under your hall. But this was highly unpleasant for the prisoner—and he was likely to be the captor next time. Soon it was the custom to treat a knightly prisoner as an honored guest. The next step was to accept a son or nephew as a hostage while the captive collected his ransom. By the thirteenth century it was usual to release a captured knight on his pledge to return if he could not raise his ransom. The early tournaments were, as has been suggested, merely arranged battles. But the knights who fought in them felt it necessary to rationalize their activity. Hence they soon believed that they fought in tournaments not for amusement or to profit by ransoms but to win glory. As time went on the tournaments were surrounded by various courteous customs, and eventually these customs developed in tournaments were carried over into actual warfare. To Froissart the Hundred Years' War was just a vast series of pleasant and amusing jousts between noble knights whose only purpose was the desire for glory. Perhaps the high point of chivalric behavior was the return of King John of France to prison in England when he found he could not raise his ransom, unless it be the action of a noble lord who hanged one of his infantrymen because he had had the bad taste to kill a knight in battle.

One more virtue of feudal chivalry requires mention: generosity. In most societies men have admired the giver of lavish gifts, and this was a marked trait among the Germans. But this virtue assumed an unusually important place in the feudal code of chivalry. Although the concepts of feudal chivalry sprang from the feudal environment, they were popularized and made universally known by professional story tellers. The evenings dragged heavily in the gloomy castles, and knights and ladies were avid for entertainment. This was supplied by various types of wanderers. There were the tellers of bawdy stories, the dancing bears, and dancing girls. But there were also trouvères who composed and recited long tales in verse and minstrels who sang the compositions of others. It was through these stories that the ideas of chivalry were spread. The livelihood of the singers and composers depended on the generosity of their patrons. Hence in their stories generosity was inclined to become the chief of all knightly virtues.

The Influence of the Church

Throughout the period in which feudalism was developing the church had consistently attempted to curb feudal warfare and turn the energies of the knights into what it considered more useful channels. The church preached vigorously its official doctrine that the taking of booty in war was sinful; on his deathbed in 1218 William Marshal complained of the rigidity of the church in this respect. In the eleventh century it decreed and tried to enforce the Truce and Peace of God, periods in which warfare was forbidden, and to protect noncombatants. It seems likely that in the minds of churchmen one purpose of the crusades was to divert knightly energy into war against the Moslems. Then in the twelfth century various ecclesiastical writers, the best known of whom was John of Salisbury, began to develop the church's conception of the perfect knight. He would be a devout Christian whose chief purpose would be to protect the church and its faith. He would faithfully serve his lawful prince. He would put down crime of all sorts and care for the weak and helpless. To strengthen its propaganda the church advanced the theory that knights formed an order like the clergy. The knight was appointed by God to fight in His service. The clergy encouraged the use of religious ceremonies in making a young man a knight and developed a complicated ritual for this purpose. The church's ideals of knightly behavior were expressed in treatises, in sermons, and also in literary works. When the noted trouvère Chrétien de Troyes wrote his *Perceval le Gallois,* he intended to depict the perfect Christian knight. A more extreme expression of the ideas of religious chivalry can be found in the stories about Galahad.

Courtly Love

The ideas of courtly love first appeared in lyric poetry composed in southern France in the second half of the eleventh century. The men and women who composed these poems were called troubadours. Scholars are not in agreement whether the origins of troubadour poetry are to be found in remnants of classical poetry preserved as folk songs or in the love poetry of the Moslems in Spain. At any rate, professional entertainers in southern France began to write poems glorifying ladies and describing the benefits to be derived from adoring them. The idea appealed to the greatest feudal prince of the region, William IX, duke of Aquitaine. Soon the composing of lyric love poems or at least the appreciation of them had become fashionable throughout southern France, the land of the *langue d'oc*. The ideas of the troubadours were few and comparatively simple. The adoration of a lady improved a man in every way. It made him a better poet, a wiser lord, and a braver knight. A lady won adoration by her beauty, her kindness, her gaiety, and her wisdom. The adorer of a lady could think of nothing but pleasing her; a slight smile from her filled him with delight. He had no interest in food and drink and was unaware whether he was hot or cold. All his thoughts and feelings were centered in his lady.

Most of the troubadour love poems were addressed to great ladies by men of comparatively humble station. If the troubadour did not want to find himself hanging from some castle tower, his adoration had to be distant and respectful, and a smile was about all the response he could expect. Presumably he was rewarded for his verse by gifts or at least by a long period of entertainment in the castle. Most of the nobles who composed poems adopted the conventions of their lesser colleagues. Hence most troubadour poetry not only glorified woman but placed her on a pedestal far above the humble lover. It is, however, interesting to notice that this idea did not occur to Duke William IX. He was a great lord and a lusty lover. No one is left in any doubt as to the reward he expected for his poems.

Troubadour poetry was not an isolated phenomenon. The same period that saw its birth and development witnessed a general rise in the status of women. The Virgin Mary, who had previously occupied a comparatively minor place in the Christian cult, became the chief intercessor with her Son for sinful man. In his youth the great Pope Innocent III wrote troubadour poems to the Virgin. In western France Robert d'Arbrissel founded a monastic order for noble women, the famous house of Fontevrault. There had, of course, always been nunneries, but they had lacked the prestige, wealth, and dignity of the great monastic foundations. Fontevrault could match in importance any monastery in the land. In short, throughout western Europe the late eleventh century saw a decided appreciation of the status of woman in the civilization as a whole.

Eleanor of Aquitaine

The ideas of courtly love spread to northern France in the train of Eleanor, duchess of Aquitaine, granddaughter of the troubadour William IX. Eleanor's first husband was King Louis VII of France, a gentle, pious man who had little appreciation for his gay and high-spirited queen and her southern attendants. When it began to appear that Eleanor would not produce a male heir for the Capetian house, Louis had the marriage annulled. Eleanor promptly married Henry, duke of Normandy and count of Anjou, who was soon to become King Henry II of England. Eleanor was a patroness of all sorts of men of letters but particularly of troubadours. One of the greatest of all the troubadours, Bernard de Ventadour, served her for many years. Her second son, Richard, known to history as the Lion-Hearted, was a patron of poets and composed some poems himself. But more important in the development of courtly love were Eleanor's two daughters by Louis VII, Marie and Alice. Marie married the most powerful and richest feudal prince of France, Henry the Liberal, count of Champagne. With plenty of money at her disposal she made her court the center for composers of works about love. Her sister Alice married Henry's younger brother, Theobald, count of Blois and Chartres, and she maintained at her court a lesser circle of literary men.

The men and women of northern France wanted something more solid than the rather vague ideas of the troubadours. If they were to sing and talk about love, they wanted to define it, examine its symptoms, and work out rules for its practice. The men of the Middle Ages were accustomed to look for the knowledge they needed in the great storehouse of classical learning. There they found a book seemingly exactly suited to their purpose, Ovid's *Art of Love*. This work was translated into French by Marie's favorite writer, Chrétien de Troyes. Another attaché of Marie's court, Andrew the chaplain, wrote a treatise on love to guide his contemporaries. Chrétien wrote a series of stories in which courtly love was an important theme. Moreover, Marie and her ladies amused themselves by holding "courts of love" at which questions dealing with the practice of this fashionable sport were debated.

The devotees of courtly love believed that they had made a great discovery and they were probably even more right than they realized. They thought that the love they were interested in had existed in classical times and had been discussed by Ovid. Now, although there are grounds for grave doubts that what we call "romantic love," the courtly love of the Middle Ages, can be found in classical literature, it is unwise to press the argument too vigorously. But there is no doubt that the love Ovid wrote about should be spelled lust. And certainly there was no romantic love in the early Middle Ages. A knight married to get a marriage portion and sons to succeed him; love did not enter into the matter. His vigorous lust was well cared for by the prostitutes who frequented the castles and by peasant girls. This conviction on the part of its devotees that courtly love was new and different led to an interesting conception, that of the incompatibility of love and marriage. A wife had to perform her marital duties, and love could never come through compulsion. This they cheerily supported by citing the ancient doctrine of the church that intercourse in marriage was justified only when there was a desire to beget children, not for mere entertainment. And the northern followers of courtly love had left far behind the conception of love as a distant admiration for a woman on a pedestal. To them love was love with no reservations.

The Courts of Love

The ideas that circulated at Marie's court are expressed largely in the treatise of Andrew the chaplain and the romances of Chrétien de Troyes. Thus Andrew discusses the interesting question as to whether or not a peasant could love. To him "No" was the obvious answer. Let a knight rape the peasant girl who caught his fancy; she could not appreciate the delicate maneuvers of the courtly lover. Then Andrew speaks of a decision by Countess Marie in her court of love. A knight had asked a lady to allow him to be her courtly lover. She had answered that she already had one, but that he could have the position if a vacancy occurred. When she married her lover, the substitute demanded that she accept him. Marie agreed with the knight. As marriage was incompatible with love, when the lady married, the position as her lover became vacant. Andrew even supplies a code of the laws of love. But perhaps the supreme expression of the courtly ideas to come from

Marie's circle is the *Lancelot* or *Le Chevalier de la charrette* of Chrétien de Troyes. Here Lancelot, the best knight in the world, renounces all that feudal chivalry prized for the sake of love. He loves Guenevere, his lord's wife, which was deep felony in feudal law. He rides in a hangman's cart, the deepest disgrace a knight could face. He allows himself to be driven ignominiously from a tournament by his opponents. He even refuses to sleep with a charming lady who offers him shelter and food when he is tired and hungry if he will be her bedmate. Thus to Lancelot all the ordinary knightly desires are of no importance; all that matters is his love for Queen Guenevere. Chrétien had his doubts about the propriety of this story. He was careful to assert that Marie had furnished the material and told him how to handle it. Soon after composing *Lancelot*, he went into the service of Count Philip of Flanders and wrote the eminently proper *Perceval*. But Lancelot remained the great hero of courtly love.

The Chansons de Geste

Before closing our discussion of chivalry, a little more extended discussion seems in order of the literature that gave expression to chivalric ideas. Feudal chivalry comes to life in the *chansons de geste*, long narrative poems. These were obviously intended for the feudal male. Their chief components are endless accounts of battles and stories of feudal intrigue. We hear how the hero hacked his foes to pieces and how he outmaneuvered them in some feudal court. Women appear only as noble mothers sending their sons to battle, as wives being beaten for indiscreet remarks, or as beautiful princesses. either Christian or Moslem, burning with desire to sleep with the hero and with no reluctance about making their wants known. Moslem princesses had one advantage from the composer's point of view: they had to be baptized eventually, and this involved undressing them and describing their charms in detail. Some *chansons de geste* had a religious element: the hero might fight the Moslems or be the benefactor of a monastery. The most beautiful of the *chansons de geste* and one of the earliest, the famous *Chanson de Roland,* is devoted almost exclusively to fighting and feudal intrigue, but the fighting was against the Moslem foes of God. Religious chivalry is best expressed in treatises by such ecclesiastics as John of Salisbury, in sermons, and in a few romances like *Perceval* and *Galahad.* We have already said a good deal about the literature of courtly love. The poems of the troubadours, those of northern poets called trouvères who wrote in the same tradition, treatises like that of Andrew the chaplain, and the romances of Chrétien de Troyes express the ideas of courtly love very fully. Then there was Marie de France, who wrote little short tales in which some of the conceptions of courtly love appear, but who was no devotee of the cult. Her *Lais,* as they were called, give us the best idea of noble life in the twelfth century that can be found in any source. Finally, we have the vast group of Arthurian stories. The basic material of the Arthurian legends was drawn from Welsh folk stories, a source used freely by Chrétien de Troyes and Marie de France. To these stories were added whatever pleased the writer. In *Lancelot* and *Tristram and Iseult* the addition is mostly courtly love. *Perceval* and *Galahad* were Welsh tales written from the point of view of religious chivalry. But a number of the Arthurian tales, perhaps the majority, bear the clear impress of the ideas of feudal chivalry. They consist of battle after battle and joust after joust. Thus if one reads through the Arthurian cycle even in its latest mediaeval form, the *Morte d'Arthur* of Sir Thomas Malory, one will find all three types of chivalry worked into the background of Welsh folklore.

CHAPTER II

The Seignorial System~~~~~~~

THE seignorial system comprised the political, social, and economic institutions that governed the lives of the agricultural workers of western Europe during the Middle Ages. As the basic function of this class was economic, the production of raw materials, the economic institutions were of primary importance. Hence the seignorial system can be understood only when it is placed in its environment: the patterns of settlement and the agricultural techniques of the period.

Speaking in broad, general terms, two patterns of settlement dominated western Europe. From the borders of Wales and Gaelic Brittany to the eastern frontier of Germany northern Europe was a land of villages. In Scotland, Wales, Gaelic Brittany, and all southern Europe the hamlet was the typical form of settlement. Thus the village system existed in the regions where the German element was strongest, and one might conclude that the Germans were its creators. But recent research has shown that over a large part of this territory the villages antedated the German settlement. This is true of northern France and parts of Germany. In England the villages were probably founded by the conquering Anglo-Saxons. There is a tendency today to credit the early peoples of western Europe with the general patterns of settlement—to suggest that the Alpine race lived in villages and the Mediterranean peoples in hamlets. But whatever the origins of the two systems, the distinction between them in the Middle Ages is clear. Although the fact that the village system covered the richest agricultural regions that were the chief centers of political power and that it was carried eastward as the Germans pushed back the Slavs makes it more important for our purpose, one must not forget that a large part of Europe was a land of hamlets.

Much the same system of cultivation prevailed over the whole village region. Each village had two or three arable fields that were cultivated in rotation. Thus in a village with two fields one would be planted and the other lie fallow. Where there were three fields, one would grow winter grain, one spring, and the third would be fallow. There is some evidence that originally all villages used the two-field system and that the three-field arrangement was an improvement developed in the more fertile districts. In addition to its arable land each village would have its waste, land almost useless, its pasture, usually fair land too steep for the plow, its meadow, and its woods. The land in the arable fields was divided into long, narrow strips. It is possible that at one time these strips were distributed each year by lot; this was often done with the meadow in the Middle Ages. But as soon as we have any adequate evidence we find the strips in the fields permanently assigned to certain tenements. A tenement would consist of a hut in the village, a fenced garden plot with perhaps a few fruit trees, an equal amount of land in each arable field, and a right to share in any use that would be made of waste, pasture, meadow, and woods. In actual practice tenements varied greatly in size, but there is reason to believe that the normal one had about a *virgate*, or thirty acres, of land in the arable fields.

The basic agricultural instrument was the heavy plow that could turn over the heavy soils of northern Europe. Apparently at first it was drawn by eight oxen, but by the twelfth century four ox teams seem to have been usual. Probably some improvement in harness made this change possible. Land was commonly measured in terms of the plow team: a *carucate* was the amount of land one team could care for while a *bovate* was the amount expected to support one ox. These oxen consumed great quantities of fodder, and one of the chief problems of mediaeval agriculture was to keep enough land under grass to supply them with pasture in the summer and hay in the winter.

Agricultural Productivity

Agricultural productivity was in general extremely low. Seed was sown broadcast to the great delight of the birds. Although by the thirteenth century it was known that seed from another district produced better results, most villages could not get it and simply used part of their own crop. The value of manure was understood, but no effective use was made of what little was available. When a crop was harvested, the cattle were turned into the field and kept on it while it lay fallow, but manuring by that method was extremely casual. And in general no village could support enough cattle to supply adequate manure. All the land that could be put under the plow was needed to supply grain for bread. Since a village had to keep enough meadow to feed its plow teams over the winter, there was little hay left over for other animals. Thus the cows lived in summer on the sparse pasture land and starved in winter. All animals not needed for breeding were usually slaughtered in the fall. The cows supplied milk that was usually turned into cheese. The sheep gave wool to make the necessary clothing. Both cows and sheep were eaten when they were slaughtered, but such occasions were rare. Moreover, the hard, rangy animals fed on the common pasture were thin and tough. A fifteenth-century writer stated that if he were forced to choose between eating a cow or its hide he would choose the hide. The most important food-producing animal was the pig. He could fend for himself winter and summer. Villages that had oak or beech woods were peculiarly fortunate because the nuts and acorns fed the swine. In England the area of a village's woodland was usually expressed in terms of the number of pigs it could feed.

Experts have calculated that a family with thirty acres in the fields and its share in wood, pasture, and meadow could probably feed itself reasonably well in good years. But the margin between the peasant and hunger was never wide, and in poor years everyone starved. The peasants' food consisted primarily of bread. To this was added some fruit and vegetables from his garden plot. Fish and chicken were rare luxuries and meat, with the exception of pork, rarer still. The well-known fat back of the southern tenant farmer was the usual meat of his mediaeval predecessor.

Until the twelfth century at least the village was essentially self-sufficient economically. It grew its own food and drink. The wool from its sheep was made into cloth by the village women. The absolutely essential craftsmen, the smith and the miller, were villagers who worked part time at those trades. The village could exist without any exchange of goods with the world beyond its borders. Although it seems likely that there was always some exchange of produce by barter, let us say one village's surplus pigs for another's surplus chickens, in general there was no market for agricultural products and hence the village had no means with which to purchase outside goods.

The Village Economy

It is important to realize that the village was far more than a group of huts surrounded by arable land, meadow, pasture, waste, and woods: it was a corporation for the exploitation of the land. The cultivation of the land was governed by the villagers as a whole. They decided when to plant, when to weed, when to harvest, what crops to grow, and what seed to use. Certain villagers were assigned specific tasks. There was a general executive to see that the common decisions were carried out. There was a hay warden who looked after the meadow and cowherds and swineherds to watch the animals in the common pasture. There was always some kind of village court to settle disputes over tenements and punish those who failed to perform their tasks.

The village was also a social and religious unit. The villagers had their festivals and celebrations. As a rule their sons and daughters married within the group. When the rural parish system was developed in the ninth and tenth centuries, the village usually became a parish with its church and priest. A group of the village elders, usually called churchwardens, looked after the fabric of the church and cared for the cemetery. In short, the village was the basic unit in mediaeval rural life.

It is more difficult to make valid generalizations about the regions where the hamlet was the pattern of settlement. In the Celtic countries what is known as the inland and outland method of cultivation was commonly used. A small

piece of land near the house would be cultivated contin-
uously and kept in a reasonable state of fertility by using
manure. At the same time a larger plot would be plowed and
used until it was worn out. Then another piece of land would
be used in the same way. This system was well adapted to
Scotland, Wales, and Brittany, where there was plenty of
very poor land. It was probably used in other similar regions. In southern France the hamlets were surrounded by
neat rectangular fields that were cultivated regularly without rotation. As the productivity must have been very low,
one must assume that the area available for each family was
correspondingly large. In general, the regions where hamlets dominated were ones of poor soil and thin population.
Except for the Celtic lands they were also deficient in rain-
fall.

The Seignorial System

Essentially the seignorial system was a set of institutions
through which the nonproductive classes, nobles and clergy,
drew their support from the agricultural workers. These
institutions varied from region to region, from district to
district, and even from village to village or hamlet to hamlet.
Their origins and development are extremely obscure. This
is partly because source materials are extremely scanty and
confusing and partly because there was no one line of development. By the twelfth century most villages were under
the domination of a lord, and the lords exploited their villages by rather similar means. Scholars have debated at
length as to whether these villages ruled by lords were originally great Roman estates worked by slaves or villages of
free German farmers that had in some way fallen under the
domination of lords. Recent research has shown that both

these theories are valid. The Roman imperial estates in Gaul passed into the hands of the Frankish kings or were given by them to the church or to their followers. Many of the great senatorial estates survived either in the hands of the descendants of their Roman owners or in those of Frankish nobles. In the late days of the empire cultivation by slaves had largely given place to cultivation by *coloni*. The *colonus* had a cottage and a small piece of land for his own use, but most of his time was devoted to working on the land reserved by the estate owner. He could not leave the estate without the owner's permission. In short, he was a semifree tenant who paid his rent for his house and plot of land by working for his lord. He was the most obvious ancestor of the mediaeval serf.

In Carolingian times we find great estates of both Roman and Frankish origin cultivated on much this same system. There is a village of tenants, and they have small plots of ground for their own use, but the major part of the land is reserved for the lord and cultivated for him by the tenants. Yet it seems clear that there were also free villages where there was no lord. Free farmers lived together and cultivated their fields in co-operation. Such villages are found in parts of England as late as the eleventh century, and they were predominant in parts of Germany. In France they probably disappeared somewhat earlier. This disappearance of free villages is not too hard to explain. In periods of violence and disorder the peasants were helpless against the knights. A village lying near a castle had little choice but to submit to the lord of the castle. If it did so, he protected it from other knights, and if it did not, he plundered it himself. Thus in times of general disorder small free farmers had only two choices: to become knights themselves or to seek the protection of a knight. And the number who could muster the resources to acquire knightly equipment must have been fairly small. Once a knight took over a village, he set up the institutions that were most effective for its exploitation, and they may well have been derived from those of the estates that had once been Roman villas.

The Demesne

Throughout most of the region of villages the seignorial system followed a common general pattern. A part of the land in the arable fields was reserved for the lord. This part, which was likely to be about a third of the total arable land, was called the demesne. The lord also reserved for himself a part of the meadow. The villagers worked the demesne for the lord: they sowed, cultivated, and harvested his grain, cut his hay, and did any other necessary work. The village herdsmen looked after the lord's cattle and swine as well as those of the villagers. If the lord wanted a moat dug for his castle or a fence built to keep deer in part of the woodland, the villagers were obliged to do it. In general, they devoted three days of the week to working for the lord, but he could require more on special occasions. Then the villagers paid the lord as rent a set proportion of the crops they grew on their own land. In addition they owed him a wide variety of payments for the use of the resources of the village lands. For pasturing their cattle they paid the lord cheeses; for letting their swine roam in the woods they paid a certain number of pigs. When the villagers fished in the stream or pond, the lord got part of the catch—usually the larger fish. In most parts of France the pike was a fish that always went to the lord.

The villagers paid rent for their tenements by working

for the lord on his demesne and by paying a wide variety of miscellaneous dues for various privileges. Then the lord usually had certain profitable monopolies. Thus usually the lord owned the mill, and the villagers were compelled to have their grain ground there. The possession of a hand mill was a serious crime. In return for grinding the grain the lord took a part of the flour. Then the lord controlled the ovens where the bread was baked and took his fee for that. In most parts of France only the lord could keep doves. They fed on the peasants' crops and were themselves eaten by the lord. Finally, the lord had a court where offenses against the rules of the village were punished. If a man tried to dodge doing the work owed the lord, if a swineherd went to sleep and lost the swine, if a villager stole apples from the lord's orchard, or if anyone was caught using a hand mill, he was tried and punished in this court.

Seignorial Jurisdiction

These various sources of revenue belonged to the lord as possessor of the land. In addition most lords had rights that they exercised in theory at least as delegates of the king. During the ninth, tenth, and eleventh centuries the powers of government that resided in the crown had been parceled out among the members of the feudal hierarchy. The beginnings of this dispersion of public authority can be found in the early days of the Germanic kingdoms. The church was accustomed to the comparatively sophisticated judicial system of the Roman Empire and had no enthusiasm for the cruder Germanic methods. Hence most bishops and abbots sought and obtained what was called immunity. When an ecclesiastical establishment had immunity, no royal official could enter its lands. In the beginning this simply meant that criminals sought by the count were seized and turned over to him by the church's officers, but as time went on there was a natural tendency to give the prelates actual powers of jurisdiction. They tended to become counts in their own lands. Unfortunately we do not know how early immunity was given to lay landholders. It seems clear that the *vassi dominici* of the Carolingian kings enjoyed this privilege. In short, in the Carolingian period the count exercised the royal power in his county as the king's delegate, but a number of lay and ecclesiastical estates were exempt from his authority and their lords exercised comtal power.

As we have seen, during the period of confusion that marked the last century of Carolingian rule, offices as well as benefices became hereditary. Thus the office of count and the right to exercise the powers of government became part of the property of a feudal family. And when a count granted part of his lands to a knight as a fief, he was inclined to grant all or part of his rights of jurisdiction. If a count wanted to persuade a very powerful landholder to become his vassal, he might well tempt him with the offer of extensive judicial powers. But probably more important than actual grants of public power was pure usurpation. A powerful feudal lord well entrenched in a strong castle was in a position to exercise what rights he pleased unless his overlord was unusually strong and determined. As the distribution of rights of jurisdiction in the feudal hierarchy depended largely on the comparative power of lords and vassals, it is difficult to make useful generalizations on the subject, but a few cautious remarks seem in order. In discussing the distribution of power in the feudal hierarchy, it was pointed out that the lowest lord who had a strong castle was likely to have the greatest relative power. This same lord was usually in possession of full royal rights of jurisdiction. The great thirteenth-century legist, Philippe de Beaumanoir, defined a baron as one "who is king in his own barony." Other contemporary writers defined a baron as the possessor of from one to three good castles. Thus throughout most of France a baron had all the rights of jurisdiction possessed by the crown; that is, his court could try all types of crimes and inflict all punishments. Lower members of the feudal hierarchy had more limited powers. By the late thirteenth century French jurists had classified rights of jurisdiction into high, middle, and low. The high justice was the full jurisdiction over all cases. The middle might have the right to hang criminals in some cases. The holder of low justice was confined to police-court jurisdiction and could use only the stocks and whipping post. In general, one can say that a lord would have at least low justice over his tenants.

It is, however, important to remember that the distribution of powers of justice varied greatly from place to place. In Normandy the duke reserved high justice for himself, and the Norman kings maintained the same system in England. Except for the so-called palatine lords—the bishop of Durham, the earls of Chester and Pembroke, and the barons of the Welsh marches—no English baron had higher powers than would have been called middle justice in France. Practically every English lord of a village had what was called *sac* and *soc*, police-court jurisdiction over his own tenants. A good many had *infangentheof*, the right to hang one of his own tenants caught in the possession of stolen goods after a hot chase. A few had *utfangentheof*, which was the privilege of hanging any man found with stolen goods on his lands. But in general all serious crimes were tried in the royal court before the king's judges.

Rights of jurisdiction were valued for three reasons. For one thing they were profitable. In minor cases one imposed money penalties. When a man was hanged, the lord having jurisdiction seized all his personal property. Then having these rights increased greatly the lord's control over his tenants. The combination of delegate of the royal judicial authority and the power of the landlord was almost impossible to resist. Finally, these rights were a mark of prestige. There were few things dearer to the heart of a mediaeval baron than his gallows; his gallows marked him as a man of position and dignity with powers of life and death over his subjects.

The Manor

The term "manor," which has deliberately been avoided in the preceding discussion as possibly confusing, properly describes the basic unit of seignorial administration. Often a manor would consist of a village and its lands, but this was by no means always true. Many villages were divided between several lords, and each one called his part a manor. Then a number of neighboring villages could be combined to form a manor. In the Celtic lands a manor could consist of a number of scattered hamlets. In certain English shires, such as Yorkshire, Lincolnshire, and Cambridgeshire, few villages had a demesne or a dominant lord. The tenants owed obligations to many different lords, some of whom had no demesne lands anywhere near the village. In this region a manor could consist of scattered tenements in many different villages. In short, a manor had only one fixed requirement: an agent of the lord who collected the rents due him and exercised his rights of jurisdiction. Thus the village was the fundamental economic and social unit of rural life; the manor was simply an artificial creation of seignorial exploitation.

The Villagers

By the eleventh century most of the people who lived in the villages were unfree. A villager could not leave his lord's land without his consent. He could not own any personal property; everything he possessed belonged to his lord. He could not marry the tenant of another lord. His lord could increase the services and rents due from the villager whenever he saw fit. But he was not a slave in the usual sense. His lord could not sell him or give him away unless he gave his tenement with him. His lord could not legally beat him or maltreat him physically. In England this distinction was very clear. The unfree villager could not bring any civil suit against his lord; he had no property rights against him. But he could carry a criminal charge against his lord to the royal courts. In France, where the lord often had full rights of jurisdiction, this distinction was probably more theoretical than practical, but it always existed. When a French baron hanged his unfree tenant, he did so as the king's delegate, not as a manorial lord. Nevertheless, the tenant had no economic rights against his lord and could be exploited at the lord's will. But here again practice probably did not follow theory too closely. The Middle Ages was a time when custom had enormous weight, and most lords probably continued to collect the same services and dues as had their ancestors, even though they had the right to increase them. Moreover, much increase was likely to be impractical. The villagers were the lord's labor force, and his land was useless to him unless they were alive and able to work.

Villain and Serf

Contemporary writers used many different terms to describe the unfree villager, and the meaning of these terms varied from region to region. Perhaps the most common was *villain*, which meant simply villager. Another was *rusticus* or countryman. In England villain was the regular term for the unfree tenant and could mean nothing else, but in France it could be used for a freeman. The word used in France to describe the unfree—and the unfree only—was *servus* or serf. Contemporary English and Norman writers insist that there were no serfs in Normandy and England, but actually there was little difference between the position of the English villain and the French serf. What difference there was sprang chiefly from the fact that in England a strong royal government protected what rights the villain had.

It is impossible to form any estimate of the relative numbers of free and unfree among the agricultural workers of the early Middle Ages. It seems that in the village region of France the peasants were almost universally unfree by the eleventh century. Although the process of reducing free villagers to serfs started later in Germany, it seems to have been equally thorough. But in England there were always freemen. While they were particularly numerous in Yorkshire, Lincolnshire, Cambridgeshire, Norfolk, and Suffolk, they existed in all parts of England. In fact, the English had a special legal term for the tenure enjoyed by the free farmer, "tenure in socage." It seems likely that freemen were more numerous in the regions where hamlets predominated. Certainly in special districts, such as the vine-growing lands and the mountainous country, they were extremely common. Most of these freemen were tenants paying rent to their lords and often owing them services. Only in a few regions, such as the country around Bordeaux, were small alodial holdings common. And all nonnoble freemen were subject to the jurisdiction of the local lord, who held delegated royal power. The tenant by knight service, the noble fief-holder, could only be tried by his fellow vassals in his lord's court, but the ordinary freeman was subject to the seignorial court.

The Great Clearing

This discussion of agriculture and the agricultural classes applies generally to the eleventh century. It now seems well to glance briefly at a few significant features of their history during the next two centuries. As a matter of fact, the eleventh century itself saw the beginnings of a tremendously important movement, what French scholars call the *grands défrichements* or the great clearing. Western Europe had never been very thickly settled. Anglo-Saxon England and the Carolingian empire had vast forests and extensive marshes that were uninhabited. The age of Viking raids and general internal confusion had greatly increased the amount of waste land. In France whole villages were deserted, and their lands reverted to the forest. The eleventh century saw the start of a vast movement of reclamation. Much of it was carefully organized by lords who hoped to exploit their fiefs more effectively. In the early eleventh century a thin populated strip of territory connected Paris and Orléans. The French kings who were lords of the region founded new villages and persuaded people to settle in them. Other lords followed similar policies. The duke of Brittany, lord of Rennes, and the barons of Fougères and Vitré turned a large part of the great forest of Rennes into rich farmland. This movement was important from several points of view.

It increased the population, the productivity of the country, and the income of the feudal lords. But it also improved the lot of the peasants. In order to attract colonists the lords offered attractive terms, and often the settlers on new lands were far better off than those who lived in older villages.

This great reclamation movement went on for at least two centuries in a wide variety of ways. Great abbeys drained marshes and cleared forests and secular lords did the same. But much of the work was on a small scale. Individual peasants got their lord's permission to clear a small tract of land and cultivate it. All along the edges of the great English forests new patches of farmland appeared. Sometimes we find traces of this process in modern place names. The Old French word for a clearing was *essart*, and in France one can find many villages with some form of this name, such as Les Essarts du Roi, or the king's clearings. More common perhaps are the names with "new" in them, Neufville, Villeneuve, and others.

The great clearing movement resulted in an expansion of the mediaeval agricultural system but did not change its essential nature. The growth of towns and the reappearance of a money economy had far more profound effects. Although these developments will be discussed in detail in the next chapter, their influence on agriculture, the agricultural classes, and the seignorial system requires mention here. Before the latter part of the eleventh century there was for all practical purposes no market for agricultural produce. The manorial lord and his household consumed what he received from his estates, and the workers consumed the rest. But as soon as towns inhabited by merchants and artisans appeared, there was a population that did not grow its own food. This immediately created a market for agricultural produce. The development of this market was a slow, gradual process. The first small merchant settlements affected only the country near at hand. Only as towns grew numerous and increased in size was a large-scale market created. As soon as this took place both manorial lords and tenants became deeply involved. Formerly a lord had no use for more produce than his household could eat; now he could sell it and buy things he wanted. The peasant could also sell his surplus on the open market. In short, money entered the agricultural economy.

The Commutation of Rents

The first change seems to have been a tendency on the part of lords and tenants to want to commute payments in kind into money rents. In the twelfth century the numerous rents still kept their ancient names, but they were usually money payments. The peasant paid a rent in money for his land in the arable fields and a sum of money for pasturing his pigs in the lord's woods. The commutation of labor services seems as a rule to have come later than that of rents, but it too was progressing in the twelfth century and became very common in the thirteenth. It was, or at least seemed to be, to the interest of both parties. The peasant resented forced labor on the demesne. The lord always wanted his hay harvested in the good weather, and it rained when the peasant had time to cut his crop. Then from the lord's point of view forced labor was incredibly inefficient. In a thirteenth-century study of estate management a large part is devoted to the means by which the tenants could be made to do their work. If the lord received money from his tenants in commutation of their labor, he could hire laborers and discharge them if they did not work. Actually, of course, the lord must have hired his own tenants, for there was no floating labor supply, but they did not have to take the work, and their lord did not have to pay them unless they worked effectively. Again, it is important to remember that commutation was a long, slow process. It probably started by the end of the eleventh century and was still uncompleted in the fourteenth. It was, however, of fundamental importance.

Closely connected with commutation was another significant movement, the freeing of the serfs. There had always been occasional enfranchisements of individuals or families. A lord might in this way reward some serf who had done him a service. The church had always preached that it was a virtuous act for a lay lord to free his serfs; a prelate could not legally do so as canon law forbade the giving away of church property. Hence once in a while a pious lord might free a number of serfs, perhaps even a whole village. But large-scale enfranchisement came only when it appeared profitable. When a lord believed that by freeing the serfs in a village he could get more revenue, he was inclined to do so. Usually the immediate consideration was a large sum of money to be paid in a fixed term. It was likely to be accompanied by higher rents than the lord had been able to collect.

Enfranchisement

When a lord freed the serfs of a village, a definite agreement, a charter of enfranchisement, was drawn up in solemn form. In it were listed all the obligations the tenants were to owe to the lord. This was in most cases simply a statement of the dues they had previously owed, though the rents might be made a little higher. The lord was careful to keep his monopolies of the mill and the oven. In general, the charter was likely to represent an economic loss rather than a

gain for the peasants. Even the rights they acquired by becoming freemen were likely to be made hard to enjoy. Thus
a free peasant could leave the lord's land, but most charters
provided that he must leave in his undershirt without taking
any personal property. The free peasant could marry when
he pleased, but he was usually required to pay a large fee if
his bride came from another lord's land.

One might ask why under such circumstances the serfs
should desire to be freed. The immediate answer is the obvious one: it was pleasant to have the prestige and position
of freeman. But probably more important was the fact that
enfranchisement ended the arbitrary economic power of the
lord. He could collect the dues set forth in the charter, but
he could not increase them. Probably neither lord nor peasants fully realized the long-range importance of this. The
early Middle Ages had been a period of economic stability,
and no one contemplated the possibility of rapid changes.
Actually, however, as the market for agricultural produce
increased, prices rose, and what was formerly a high rent
became a small one. In short, once rents had been commuted
and fixed by a charter, the lord was the loser if any inflation
took place. The nobles of France were hard hit by the de-
basement of the coinage carried out by the fourteenth-
century kings. A large proportion of them were ruined by
the inflation of the fifteenth and sixteenth centuries.

The Disappearance of the Demesne

One more important development of the thirteenth and
fourteenth centuries requires mention. When a lord commuted the labor services of his tenants, he was obliged to
work his demesne with hired labor. This was a good deal of a
nuisance. He had to have efficient managers and account-

ants and auditors to keep track of them. Moreover, he did not as a rule actually want the produce of the demesne. The produce of the village adjoining his residence and perhaps that of a few neighboring estates was used to feed his household. What was grown on the demesnes of his other manors was sold. In short, the lord wanted money rather than grain. Soon it occurred to him that it would be much simpler to stop cultivating his demesne himself and to rent it out to tenants. Here too, of course, the process was slow and gradual. But in general one can say that by the end of the thirteenth century many lords were no longer directly engaged in agriculture; they were simply landlords who collected rents. During the fourteenth and fifteenth centuries their number increased very rapidly. By the sixteenth century the demesne was a thing of the past in most of France and England.

CHAPTER III

The Development of
Towns and Commerce

DURING the last twenty years there has been extensive discussion of the history of commerce and urban life in the early Middle Ages. Scholars have disagreed strongly, sometimes rather violently. These debates have centered essentially on quantitative questions: How much trade and urban life were there at various times? If one wanted to draw a chart showing commercial activity between the fifth and the eleventh centuries, there would be fairly general agreement as to the general curve but considerable disagreement as to the quantity of activity represented by any one point. We cannot here discuss the arguments used, much less enter into the debate. We must content ourselves with describing the general curve and making a few remarks about the state of urban life and commercial activity in the late tenth and early eleventh centuries.

In the western part of the Roman Empire the high point of urban and commercial development was probably reached in the first and second centuries after the birth of Christ. By the third century the civil wars resulting from the struggles of rival candidates for the imperial crown had reduced the level of prosperity. By the fourth century both Gaul and Britain were suffering from Germanic raids. The heavy taxation that gradually ruined the middle class was a severe blow to urban life. Thus when the German invaders entered the empire in large numbers in the fifth century, they found commerce already sadly decayed and the urban centers weak and depopulated. The establishment of the Germanic states did not halt this process but rather accelerated it. The Germans were unused to town life and had no desire to become accustomed to it. The Germanic kings had no interest in keeping roads and bridges in repair and safeguarding merchants. There seems to be no doubt that trade declined steadily and town life gradually disappeared. The cities along the coast of the Mediterranean were to some extent at least an exception. Until the eighth century there was nothing to hinder commerce on that sea, and such cities as Narbonne appear to have remained important trading centers. Then in the eighth and ninth centuries the Moslems conquered Spain, the Balearic Islands, Corsica, Sardinia, and Sicily. Moslem fleets were in complete control of the western Mediterranean. Although it is most unlikely that commerce ceased entirely, as far as the Christian states were concerned it became so slight as to be of little significance.

The Decline of Commerce

In the tenth century commercial activity in western Europe was at its lowest ebb. There was very little contact with the great trading centers of the Near East. The Byzantine fleet kept open a tenuous line of communication with Venice and a few other towns on the Adriatic coast of Italy. Once the Swedish Vikings had established themselves in Russia, they conducted trade with both Constantinople and

Bagdad, but all that seeped through to the west were a few articles of gold and silver and some coins. Within western Europe itself there must, of course, always have been some trade. Certainly the knights of this region did not have all their equipment made and their war horses bred locally. But it is clear that what commerce there was, was so slight in amount that it played no part of any significance in the life of the time. Merchants were extremely few, and very little money was in circulation. In general, each community was economically self-sufficient.

It seems unlikely that any towns in the economic sense existed in western Europe during the tenth century. There were, of course, conglomerations of buildings, usually on the site of an ancient town. Every bishop had his city with its cathedral, episcopal palace, residences for the cathedral clergy, and houses for the various people who served the church and its clergy. At Paris the Ile de la Cité contained a royal residence in addition to the ecclesiastical buildings. At Rouen three centers of population lay in close juxtaposition: the ducal tower of Rouen, the cathedral, and the great monastery of St. Ouen. At Tours there was the seat of the counts of Touraine, the cathedral, and the monasteries of St. Martin and Marmoutier. Thus a good many ancient towns had a fair number of people living on their sites. But these people were not primarily merchants and artisans. They were tenants of manorial lords who grew their food in the fields near at hand. For example, at Rouen there were three villages surrounding the residences of three lords, the duke of Normandy, the archbishop of Rouen, and the abbot of St. Ouen. Once again it is important to emphasize that these places probably contained some men who were engaged in trade. There were almost certainly people living on the riverbank on the Ile de la Cité at Paris whose chief occupation was transporting goods on the Seine, and the same was probably true of Rouen. But these people and their activities were of little or no significance in the economic life of the period.

The Revival of Trade

The eleventh century saw the reversal of the downward trend of commercial activity and the reawakening of urban life in western Europe. Because of the small amount of material available to the historian, this development will always remain obscure in detail. One can merely point out the conditions necessary for commerce and urban life and mention various indications that these existed and were taking effect in the eleventh century. The basic requirement for the existence of commerce is that each of two groups of people produce a surplus of a different commodity and that each wants what the other produces. It is also necessary that it be possible to transport the surplus of each group to the location inhabited by the other at a cost that is consistent with the desire for the commodity. Then if the trade is to rise above the level of mere barter, there must be a medium of exchange acceptable to both groups: normally, coined money. Finally, there must be people able and willing to carry on the trade.

In the eleventh century several districts of western Europe were producing a surplus of commodities for which there was a demand elsewhere. Probably the most important of these districts was the county of Flanders. There is some evidence that as early as the Carolingian period this district produced woolen cloth of unusually fine quality. By the middle of the eleventh century it was making more than could be used locally. Another district that produced commodities for which there was a general demand was the forest of the far north. Trade between the north and Flanders was easy. Norse merchants could load their ships with honey, furs, and hunting hawks, sail down to Flanders, and exchange their cargo for woolen cloth, for which there was an active demand in the north. Then the Flemish merchants could peddle the furs, hawks, honey, and their own cloth among the aristocracy of northern France and Germany. They may well have been paid largely in raw wool. Thus Flanders became the first industrial and commercial center of western Europe.

Another important commerce was started apparently by the creation of a demand. In France wine was the usual drink of the people of every class, and each district produced enough for its own local needs. But there were parts of the country peculiarly suited to the culture of the vine that could easily produce surpluses if a demand appeared. The Anglo-Saxons were ale drinkers, and wine was not made in England. When in the reign of Edward the Confessor England began to swarm with his Norman friends, these Normans wanted the wine to which they were accustomed. We know little in detail about the wine trade in the eleventh century, but it is clear that before the Norman Conquest merchants from Rouen appeared regularly in London. The Conquest, of course, enormously increased this demand for wine in England. Wine coming from northern Burgundy was shipped down the Seine to Rouen and thence to England. After the accession to the English throne of Henry II, already count of Anjou and duke of Aquitaine, the vineyards of the Loire valley and those of the Bordeaux region entered into competition with those of Burgundy for the English market.

Before the Norman Conquest of England Norman merchants had played a part in the slow development of commerce in northern France, and many of them followed Duke William to his new kingdom. England had a number of products that were in demand on the continent. The tin mines of Devon and Cornwall had been known to the Phoenicians and had been actively exploited by the Romans. The Norman kings encouraged tin mining by giving the miners special privileges to facilitate the pursuit of their trade, and they organized the commerce in the tin produced into a tight governmental monopoly. The lead miners of Derbyshire and Cumberland were encouraged in the same way. England was the only source of tin in western Europe and an important producer of lead and silver. Then by the late eleventh century the weavers of Flanders were having difficulty finding the raw wool they needed, and England even before the Conquest had a great number of sheep. Soon the Flemings were relying heavily on England for their wool supplies, and England was increasing her production to meet the demand. The first great expansion in English woolgrowing seems to have come with the appearance of the Cistercian monks in the twelfth century. The Cistercians were bound by their rule to refuse to accept land that was already inhabited. They were to support themselves by their own labor, not by that of their tenants. Before long great tracts of inarable land in Yorkshire, Lincolnshire, the borders of Wales, and other regions were given to the Cistercians by the English barons. They soon discovered the desirability of using it as sheep pasture. By this means wild, waste land could with little expenditure of labor be made highly profitable. In a short time secular lords in the same districts were emulating the Cistercians, and England became the center of woolgrowing for all western Europe.

While a flourishing commerce with its chief center in Flanders was slowly spreading over northwestern Europe, an equally, perhaps more, important development was taking place in the south. Early in the eleventh century the western towns of north Italy headed by Genoa and Pisa began to build ships and to trade along the Mediterranean shores to the west. To protect this commerce they organized a series of expeditions against the Moslems who held Corsica and Sardinia. Meanwhile Venice had become independent politically but still maintained an active trade with Constantinople. Her fleet was mistress of the Adriatic Sea. In addition, certain inland towns, notably Milan in Lombardy and Florence in Tuscany, had become important centers for the weaving of woolen cloth. Northern Italy was ready for any commercial opportunities that might appear.

The Influence of the Crusades

This opportunity came with the First Crusade. The great crusading army of heavily armed knights marched overland to Constantinople and on through Asia Minor to the Holy Land. There they established the Latin kingdom of Jerusalem. Most of Palestine and a large part of Syria became a state organized on feudal lines and ruled by barons from western Europe. The kingdom of Jerusalem needed supplies of all sorts from Europe. Moreover, great numbers of individual crusaders and pilgrims wanted transportation to the Holy Land. Hence there was a large immediate demand for shipping. Genoa and Pisa rose to this need and carried the supplies and men in their ships. To protect this shipping from the Moslem fleets they organized squadrons of warships that soon won effective control of the Mediterranean.

From the latter part of the eleventh century to the appearance of the Ottoman Turks as a naval power in the fifteenth century, the fleets of Genoa, Pisa, and Venice were masters of the great inland sea.

The kings of Jerusalem and their barons were fully aware that the very existence of their state depended on the ships of the Italian cities. They gave the Italian merchants extensive trading privileges throughout the kingdom. Soon the caravan routes to Damascus were swarming with goods bound for the Italian merchants operating in the Latin kingdom. The most important of these commodities were silken cloths, sugar, and a wide variety of spices. These goods were loaded on Italian ships and carried back to Italy. Thus once more the luxury goods produced in the east became available in the southern part of western Europe. In short the end of the eleventh century saw active trading centers in both Flanders and Italy.

The Secondary Needs of Trade

The eleventh century also saw some development in the secondary needs of active commerce. Although there is no evidence that there was any improvement in methods of transportation, the efforts of the church and the great feudal princes were gradually making the roads and rivers safer for commercial travel. The merchant still had to pay tolls at every castle he passed and he always ran the risk of having his goods seized by a greedy baron, but some semblance of order began to appear. Then mining operations were rapidly increasing the silver available for coining money. The Norman kings of England obtained some silver from their lead mines, but the chief development was the opening of the rich Saxon silver mines near Goslar and their active exploitation by Emperors Henry III and Henry IV. It was largely German silver that supplied the currency for the growing trade. Finally, a merchant class was slowly growing. Here there is almost no evidence as to just what took place. It can only be assumed that men saw an opportunity and were adventurous enough to seize it. A large proportion of these men must have been unfree peasants who deserted their lords to become peddlers who wandered over the countryside. But this was only the beginning. As we shall see, the growing towns soon supplied an adequate merchant class.

If a man was to engage in trade effectively he required certain things. Perhaps the most important of these was personal freedom and some lord who would vouch for him as a freeman. Obviously one who could not leave his lord's land could not operate as a merchant, and a runaway serf without credentials was at the mercy of any knight who desired his goods. A merchant also needed a house to live in and a shop or small warehouse to hold his goods, and it was important that the rent for them be payable in the product of his business, money. He could not perform labor services for his lord to pay for his tenement. Then if he was to engage in trade with any enthusiasm, he had to have some assurance that his money and goods would not be taken from him by his lord. All the dues he owed had to be fixed amounts that the lord could not increase at will. He needed a guarantee that his lord would not take advantage of some minor offense he committed to levy a ruinous fine on him. Finally, a merchant wanted the right to form a co-operative organization with his neighbors. Only thus could he achieve reasonable security. If he lost his goods, the association would help him start again. It would care for his family and see to his burial when he died. If a merchant in some other town did not pay him the money due him, the association would help him recover it.

Town Charters

The early merchants looked for places to live where the location was suitable for trade and where the local lord was willing to give them the privileges they needed. Usually they settled near a castle, an abbey, or an episcopal city. In Paris the merchant colony grew up on the right bank of the Seine opposite the Ile de la Cité. At Lincoln the merchants lived on a steep slope that ran from the cathedral, bishop's palace, and royal castle down to the river Witham. Soon most well-located castles, abbeys, and cathedrals had their *faubourg*, or merchant settlement. The merchants would approach the lord of the place and ask him for a charter of privileges. Sometimes they would offer him a large sum of money, sometimes an attractive annual income, and often both. The lord would then grant them a charter. Rarely were two town charters exactly alike, though various lords had model charters that they followed fairly closely. But while variety in detail was endless, the basic privileges mentioned in the last paragraph were always included. The land of the merchant settlement became free land; anyone who lived there for a year and a day became a freeman. The lord usually excepted from this provision his own serfs, but he was glad to receive the escaped serfs of other lords. The merchants would owe fixed money rents for their tenements. This was usually called burgage tenure to distinguish it from other methods of holding land. Then the special dues the lord was to demand were usually fixed. The lord could ask for so much a year in tallage and for a further sum to persuade him not to debase his coinage. Often the charter listed the money penalties that the lord could collect for various offenses. In addition the charter usually gave the merchants the right to form a guild or co-operative association. When the guild was not mentioned in the charter, it was usually because it already existed. In many cases the merchants formed a guild and the guild carried out the negotiations for the charter.

The privileges mentioned above were the fundamental ones, those that were absolutely necessary for a community of merchants. Many, perhaps most, towns obtained other rights in the original or subsequent charters. Trade was bound to involve numerous disputes about debts, agreements, quality of goods, and such questions. The lord's officers knew nothing about such matters. Hence usually the merchants were allowed to hold a court to decide commercial cases. Then if the lord was feeling generous or was offered a very attractive sum of money, he might allow the merchants' court to dispense police-court or low justice while his officers kept the higher jurisdiction. Such was the situation in Paris. The elected head of the guild, the provost of the merchants, had a court for commercial questions and low justice, but all important cases went to the king's provost of Paris. Some towns had still higher privileges. Many English towns induced the king to allow the guild and its officers to take over local government and collection of the king's dues. They were subject to the general supervision of the sheriff of the county, but there was no royal officer in the town itself. London was a county in itself and had its own elected sheriffs. In France many towns achieved almost complete independence. They were governed by an elected mayor assisted by elected aldermen. The mayor had full rights of jurisdiction: both high and low justice. The lord had the right to a fixed sum of money from the town every year, but otherwise he had no rights over it.

Towns and Feudalism

A flourishing town was a valuable asset to a feudal lord. For one thing it brought him a large income in the form of money. Then most towns had a well-equipped and reasonably well-drilled militia. Although these troops were infantry and hence not of much use in the field against knights, they were able to defend their own walls and thus gave the lord an extra garrisoned fortress. Moreover, towns were useful for the purpose of increasing the population of one's lands at the expense of a neighbor. In the twelfth century the king of France and the count of Champagne carried on a town-founding race along their mutual frontier in order to steal each other's serfs. The desirability of towns made lords anxious to have as many as possible. Often a feudal prince would give a charter to a location that seemed promising in the hope that a town would spring up. But from the point of view of the lords, the basic privileges of personal freedom for the inhabitants, burgage tenure, fixed dues and fines, the right to have a guild, and perhaps a court for commercial cases and low justice was all a town should have. Very rarely did a lord voluntarily give a town greater powers of self-government. The towns that had more advanced privileges usually won them by rebellion against weak lords. In France and Italy such towns were often called "communes." A commune was fundamentally simply a sworn alliance of a group of people associated for a stated purpose, in this case revolt against the lord. Some rural villages formed such alliances and won special rights. But usually the commune was an association of townsmen working together for greater self-government. The king of France would not allow communes in his own lands, but he was glad to encourage them in the lands of his vassals. A large proportion of the French communes were in towns ruled by a bishop such as Beauvais. The bishop usually had trouble mustering enough troops to put down a revolt, and when the king supported the rebels, he was utterly helpless. The communes of Italy were basically similar to those of France except that they represented an alliance of merchants and lesser nobles against the bishop who ruled the town. The minor nobles of the countryside moved into the town and joined the merchants in forcing the bishops to give them self-government. In Germany the great towns were given extensive political privileges by the emperor, who hoped to use them to curb the power of the nobles.

Overland Routes

For the further development of commerce and urban life in western Europe, following the eleventh and early twelfth century revival discussed above, one principal need was a connecting link between Italy and Flanders. This was no simple task. The Moslem fleets controlling the waters around the Strait of Gibraltar and the storms of the Bay of Biscay and the English Channel made the sea route far too hazardous for twelfth-century merchants. The land routes passed through the lands of innumerable feudal lords who expected to be paid tolls if they restrained themselves from plundering the traveling merchants. But it was, in fact, the enterprise of a powerful feudal prince that finally supplied the needed link. Geographically the easiest and most natural land route from the Mediterranean to northern France was up the valleys of the Rhône and Saône to eastern France. This region was equally well connected with the north. The Moselle led to the Rhine, the tributaries of the Seine to Paris, Rouen, and England, and the Loire to western France. Thus geographically the region we call Champagne was ideally situated as a meeting place between the traders of the north and the south. In the twelfth century this region was under the control of the most powerful of French feudal houses: the counts of Champagne, Blois, and Chartres. These counts, particularly Henry the Liberal, who ruled from 1152 to 1181, were fully aware of the advantages of their position and the profits they could draw from it.

The Fairs of Champagne

At a number of the chief towns of their domains, notably Troyes, Provins, and Lagny-sur-Marne, the counts of Champagne founded fairs. These fairs were so spaced that there was usually one of them going on. The counts saw that everything necessary was supplied. There were booths to be rented to merchants, money-changers to handle the many diverse types of coin that the traders brought in, police to keep order, and judges to give quick decisions in disputes. All this was highly profitable to the count. In addition to the rents for the booths, the percentage taken by the money-changers, and the fines for offenses committed at the fair, he charged a sales tax on all goods brought to the fair. The fairs were carefully organized. Each day was devoted to commerce in a different type of commodity. Thus on one day only furs and hides would be dealt in, on another textiles. During the days of trade no money actually changed hands, but careful accounts were kept in the official money of the fair, the silver pound of Troyes and Provins. Then on the last day all the accounts were settled with the aid of the money-changers.

Fully as important as the local arrangements was the protection supplied by the counts to merchants bound for their fairs. No merchant could be arrested at the fair or anywhere in the count's lands while he was going to or coming from a fair for any debt except those contracted at one of the fairs. In addition the count through his vassals was able to supply protection along the routes leading to the fair. Many of the lesser lords of northern France, such as the counts of Dreux and Soissons, held fiefs from the count of Champagne. Then to safeguard the long route along the valleys of the Rhône and Saône the count gave money fiefs, in other words regular pay, to a number of powerful barons of the region. They did homage, swore fealty, and promised to protect the merchants. In return they were paid from the proceeds of the fairs. The counts used the same system to extend their influence into the German duchy of Lorraine. Thus by the end of the twelfth century merchants bound for the fairs of Champagne found most of their routes watched over by the count or his vassals.

The fairs of Champagne were extremely successful. Italian merchants bearing the rare goods of the east went there to buy raw wool, furs, hides, and other products of northern Europe. The merchants of the north went there to buy the goods of the east to distribute in their own countries. But these fairs were more than what we would call wholesale markets. The great lords of France would send their stewards to the fairs to buy their year's supply of sugar, spices, fine textiles, rich furs, and military equipment. When the English knight, William Marshal, found himself in need of a new war horse, he went to the fair of Lagny to buy it.

While the fairs of Champagne were the most important centers of trade in western Europe in the twelfth and early thirteenth centuries, other fairs sprang up rapidly. Most of these were chiefly local in scope. Merchants would buy the goods of the east and Flemish cloth at the fairs of Champagne and then sell them by wandering from one local fair to another. A few were noted for particular products. Thus Boston in eastern England was the natural outlet for a flourishing wool-growing region and became a great center for trade in raw wool. To it journeyed merchants from Flanders and even from the weaving towns of Italy. The English kings bought a large part of their household supplies at Boston fair. In short, during the twelfth and thirteenth centuries a large part of what we call foreign trade was carried on at the fairs. They ranged in size and importance from the great fair of Troyes to the annual fair at the chief seat of some petty feudal lord, the latter being basically an annual cattle market where some peddlers with rare goods might be found.

The Hanseatic League

Late in the thirteenth century the fairs of Champagne began to lose their position. Their decline was the result of a number of developments. Champagne had come by marriage into the possession of the Capetian house, and the kings were too greedy. By raising the rents and taxes at the fairs they drove merchants elsewhere. But more serious was the appearance of competing routes. By the late thirteenth century the kings of Germany were almost powerless and were completely unable to control the princes. Hence the imperial cities, often called the free cities, formed leagues for mutual protection. A group of North German towns headed by Lübeck made an alliance called the Hanseatic League. They combined to put pressure on the princes to protect their merchants, to maintain warships to check piracy, and to operate trading stations. One of the most famous of these stations was the Steelyard in London. The League made arrangements with other free cities throughout Germany and thus developed an overland route to Italy. From the cities of North Germany the routes ran to Ulm and Augsburg and from there over the Alpine passes into Italy. During the fourteenth century these routes captured most of the trade between Italy and the north. What commerce did use the Rhône-Saône route found its entrepôt at Lyons. That city became the chief commercial town of France and had a very important fair.

The Craft Guilds

As time went on various changes took place in the institutional structure of most towns. Perhaps the most important of these was the development of the craft guilds. When a town was founded, there was only one guild, and all the inhabitants were members of it. Its officials were the governing body of the town and exercised all the powers granted by the charter. But this situation did not usually last very long. The members of the guild who enjoyed its privileges were inclined to be hesitant about admitting new members. Serfs could flee to the town, live there a year and a day, and so become freemen, but they were fortunate if they obtained membership in the guild. Soon most towns had an unprivileged population. Then great differences in wealth and economic interests began to develop among the members of the guild itself. The merchants who lived by trade were likely to make far more money than the artisans. As they made their money by importing goods into the town and selling them to their fellow citizens, they were interested in using their monopoly to keep prices high. This annoyed the artisans, who had no part in the profits. Hence bit by bit the artisans broke away from the town guild and formed their own separate corporations. The process differed somewhat from town to town. In Oxford the town guild remained the dominant one and the others were simply subordinate guilds. No one could belong to an occupational guild who was not a member of the town guild. But in most towns there was a complete separation. The original guild became the merchant guild and the craftsmen left it to form their own organizations.

The formation of the craft guilds was a long, slow process that extended over many years. By the end of the twelfth century the only craft guilds found in England outside London were those of the textile workers: weavers, dyers, and fullers. In parts of France the guild structure seems to have developed a little earlier, but it is not until the thirteenth century that it appeared in full flower. Almost every conceivable occupation was represented by a guild. There were butchers', bakers', swordmakers', goldsmiths', tanners', leatherworkers', booksellers' and parchment-makers' guilds. In some French cities, notably Paris and Toulouse, the prostitutes had a guild. As a rule the members of a guild tended to live together on the same street.

Guild Regulations

The primary purpose of the craft guild was to safeguard the economic interests of its members. No artisan could work in a town unless he was a member of the local guild, and goods could not be imported into a town if they competed with local products. Thus each guild had a monopoly of the market in its own town. The guild also did everything possible to prevent competition among its members. It laid down detailed regulations governing the quality of its product, the methods of manufacture, and the price that could be charged for it. The ideal was to have every member of the guild make exactly the same thing by the same methods and sell it at the same price. Hours of labor were rigidly controlled. Thus in difficult trades requiring careful work no one could labor before sunrise or after sunset.

Obviously this closely controlled monopoly would only work effectively if the supply of products was fairly well adjusted to the demand. Each guild tried to do this by limiting the number of its members. Before a young man was admitted to the guild, he had to learn the trade by serving as an apprentice to a guild member or master. The guild set the number of apprentices each member could have and the number of years they had to serve in that capacity. Thus the guild could control the number of craftsmen in its occupation. It also made sure that its members were adequately trained. When an apprentice had served his time, he had to produce a "masterpiece" for the inspection of the guild's officers to prove his ability to practice his trade.

In the early days of a craft guild each member had a small workshop where he labored with a few apprentices, and when an apprentice finished his term, he became a master and had his own shop. But there was a natural inclination on the part of the masters who were the members of the guild to keep their numbers down, have more workmen under them, and thus increase their profits. Before long an apprentice could not become a master as soon as he finished his term of training; he had to work for a certain number of years as a journeyman or hired day laborer. In this way masters could have fairly large shops where apprentices and journeymen worked for them. As time went on the members of the guild became more and more disinclined to increase their number and reduce each one's share of the market. They preferred as the market grew to take more apprentices. Eventually it became almost impossible to become a master unless you were the son of a master or married a master's daughter. The majority of men working in the craft could not hope to rise beyond journeyman.

The journeymen were pretty completely at the mercy of the masters who ran the guild. The guild guaranteed every journeyman work. In Paris the journeymen of a guild gathered each morning at a certain place. The masters came and chose the men they wanted, but if there were some left when the choosing was over, the guild officers assigned them to masters. Through the guild, however, the masters set the journeyman's wages and regulated the hours and conditions of his work. In some towns the journeymen attempted to form organizations of their own to fight the masters, but as the latter always had the support of the town government, the journeymen were rarely successful.

The craft guilds could obviously abuse their monopolies to the detriment of their fellow citizens, by lowering the quality of their goods and by raising the price. In England where the royal government was strong the more important guilds were carefully supervised. From at least the reign of King John the English government set the weight, quality, and price of loaves of bread and the quality and measure of ale. Later when cloth began to be an important manufacture, strict regulations for its making were laid down and were enforced by governmental inspectors. In France the guilds were likely to be strictly controlled in cities where the lord was powerful. Thus in Paris the regulations of most guilds had to be approved by the royal provost of Paris and he was responsible for seeing that the guild officers enforced them. Other guilds were controlled by various dignitaries. The booksellers and inkmakers, for example, were ruled by the rector of the university, the makers of candles and sacred vestments by the bishop, and the wine dealers by the royal butler. But in self-governing towns control was difficult, and the guilds tended to abuse their monopolies rather freely.

Social Services of the Guilds

Although the chief purpose of the guilds was economic, they had social and religious functions as well. They cared for the widows and children of members who died and paid the costs of the funeral. Often they ran schools for the children of their members. Each guild had a patron saint, and the guild conducted religious ceremonies in his or her honor. Usually the religious functions of the guild were performed by a separate organization called a *confrérie*, but its members were the members of the guild. The religious interests of the guilds are illustrated particularly well by the great nave windows at Chartres cathedral, each of which was donated by one of the town's guilds.

The rise of the craft guilds brought serious political disturbances in many cities. The members of the merchant guild who controlled the town government were naturally disinclined to give it up, and the craft guilds were equally unwilling to leave the merchants in power. The result in many places was riots and revolts. In Flanders in the fourteenth century the craftsmen rebelled, overthrew the government of the rich merchants, and routed in pitched battle the merchants' ally, the king of France. Later they formed an alliance with Edward III of England. Few revolts of craftsmen made as much commotion as that of the Flemish weavers, but there were serious risings in many towns. As a rule they were terminated by some arrangement that gave the craft guilds a share in the town government.

The guild system had many obvious advantages. It provided a large measure of social and economic security for guild members. It also supplied the means for guild members to co-operate for all sorts of activity—social, economic, and political. The great weakness of the system was its inability to adjust itself to technological progress. No guild member could use a new method of manufacture until it had been accepted by the guild as a whole and provided for in the regulations. Such acceptance was in practice almost impossible. Hence from very early times innovators were forced to work outside the jurisdiction of the guilds. Thus in the twelfth century the regular method of fulling cloth was to put it in water and stamp on it or beat it with paddles. Late in the century it occurred to someone that water power could do this more effectively, and fulling mills began to appear. But the guilds refused to have anything to do with them. The fulling mills were built outside the towns away from the jurisdiction of the guilds, usually on the land of a noble so powerful that the guilds dared not refuse to accept the product of his mills. In general this was the story of later technological improvements. Much of the wool industry of late mediaeval England grew up in the countryside to avoid the guilds.

The Growth of Towns

While there were, of course, vast differences between various mediaeval towns, a few general remarks seem in order. As we have seen, most towns began as a merchant settlement adjoining a castle, abbey, or episcopal city. At first the inhabitants relied on the castle, abbey, or city for shelter in time of danger, but as the town grew in population and wealth they were inclined to fortify it with walls. As the building of a wall was extremely expensive, as small an area as possible was enclosed. Hence space within the shelter of the walls was always at a premium and was used to the fullest possible extent. The result was narrow streets with the upper floors of the houses built out over them. There were, of course, no public sanitary arrangements, and refuse of all sorts was simply dumped in the streets. Although paving of streets was not unknown, it was extremely rare because of its cost. If a town was growing rapidly, the space within the walls was soon exhausted and settlements sprang up outside. When these suburbs grew sufficiently important the walls might be extended to include them. In Paris the various stages in the gradual enlargement of the walled enclosure can still be traced in the street names. Thus the rue St. Honoré becomes the rue du Faubourg St. Honoré.

Religious Life

The dominance of religion in the life of the people of the Middle Ages was particularly apparent in the towns. There were an incredible number of churches; London had 120 about 1200. If the town adjoined an episcopal city, the cathedral dominated the landscape, and its size and splendor was the chief pride of the townsmen. In fact the magnificent cathedrals built in the twelfth and thirteenth centuries are the most striking monument to the civic pride of the towns. But in addition to its cathedral a town of any importance would have a number of monastic establishments and collegiate churches and many simple parish churches. Thus from a distance a mediaeval town was a cluster of church towers and spires. Next to the churches the chief architectural feature of the town was likely to be one or more castles. These were usually situated so that they could be defended against the inhabitants of the town as well as against an outside foe; usually they were astride the town walls. Thus the Tower of London dominated the town on the eastern side while Barnard's Castle overlooked it from the west. When King Philip Augustus built the great fortress of the Louvre, it was situated at the edge of the merchant settlement of Paris. Late in the fourteenth century the Bastille was built at the opposite end of the town. In addition two small fortresses, the Chatelets, held the bridgeheads leading from the Ile de la Cité to both banks of the Seine and served as seats of the royal provost of Paris. The Tower of London, the Louvre, the Bastille, and the Chatelets were strongholds belonging to the overlord of the town, but Barnard's Castle belonged to an English baron, and private strongholds were common in towns. In Winchester the bishop as well as the king had a castle, and in Lincoln one of the bishop's vassals had a small fortress. In Italy where the nobles of the countryside resided in the town such urban strongholds were very numerous. Rome was dotted with the towers of fortresses held by such families as the Orsini and Colonna. Outside the churches and fortresses, public buildings were few. Every town had its town hall, often called the guildhall, and sometimes the craft guilds had halls of their own. In important and rich cities such as London and Bruges, the guildhalls were magnificent buildings, but in most towns they were modest affairs.

The Administration of Justice

Most mediaeval towns had within their limits a wild mixture of jurisdictions. Thus in Paris the royal provost had high justice over the merchant town on the right bank of the Seine while the provost of the merchants had low justice. On the Ile de la Cité the bishop had full rights of justice except in the immediate vicinity of the royal palace. On the left bank lay the university, and justice there was divided between the Abbots of Sainte Geneviève and Saint-Germain-des-Prés. In all towns where a bishop had his seat the episcopal city was under his direct control rather than that of the regular town government. In addition to these general jurisdictions there were many special ones. Usually a monastic establishment had special privileges extending over its property. In London the Knights Templars had a "liberty" into which the city officials could not enter. When the lord had a castle in the town, its constable usually had jurisdiction over a section of the town adjacent to the castle. In short, the same complications that existed in seignorial government in the countryside found their way into the towns.

The Inhabitants of the Towns

The inhabitants of the towns formed a new class in mediaeval society; they were neither nobles nor peasants. Their occupation demanded that they have some education. They had to be able to read and write and know some arithmetic. This made them well fitted to become the officials of the feudal princes. Their ideas and way of life were necessarily different from that of the nobles. As they devoted their time to trade and industry, they were not trained soldiers and had as a rule little taste for war. Hence the nobles to whom war was the only worthy occupation were inclined to scorn them. Then the chivalric virtue of generosity required the noble to be free with his money, jewels, and other movable property. This was easy enough for the noble because such property represented income, not capital—his capital was his land. But the townsman's capital was largely movable property, actual money and goods. If he was to survive he had to be careful with it. As a result the townsmen were considered grasping and stingy. But most of the ill-feeling between noble and townsman probably came from the fact that the latter could live as comfortably as, if not more so than, the noble. He could afford rich clothes, fine silver service, jewels, and rich foods. He had an abundance of what the noble usually lacked—ready money. In short, the noble saw a group of men sprung largely from peasants with what he considered lowly tastes and ideals competing with him in magnificence of life.

A Just Price

Before leaving the subject of the development of towns and commerce, it seems well to discuss a few closely connected topics. Perhaps the most important of these concerns the ideas of the time regarding commerce and commercial practices. In the early Middle Ages when trade was relatively undeveloped ecclesiastical writers were doubtful whether the pursuits of commerce were compatible with a life of virtue which led to eventual salvation. By the twelfth and thirteenth centuries, however, churchmen recognized the social importance of men of commerce and provided a full-scale moral justification of their activities. Merchants who avoided fraud, contributed honest labor, and sought profit to support themselves and their families were worthy of praise. Only those who cheated, performed no labor or were motivated by insatiable greed were morally suspect. Concurrently the doctrine of the "just price" was developed. By the time of Thomas Aquinas in the thirteenth century a price was considered just if it roughly corresponded to the going price, that is, the current market value. Somewhat later as municipal price regulation increased a second criterion was added. Prices must also conform to legally fixed rates where this regulation was applicable. Prices were only unjust where one gained from another's special disadvantage in individual bargains to force a price which differed from the free market or legal value.

The church steadfastly refused to give its approval to a number of practices that we take as a matter of course. What we call speculation was forbidden by canon law and by the regulations of most secular governments. Thus it was generally agreed that it was sinful to buy something, keep it for a time in the same place, and then out of a motive of pure greed sell it at a higher price. Usury was also banned by the church. As usury was defined as the taking of any interest for money given as a loan, this theoretically made money lending and many forms of banking impossible as occupations for Christians. In the early Middle Ages the profession of money lender was confined to Jews, who were not bound by church law. Later on, however, the ecclesiastical censures were directed primarily against manifest usurers or petty pawnbrokers. Other forms of banking transactions and business arrangements which disguised usury were frequently unmolested. For example, in the thirteenth century we find an Italian merchant lending money to the English government under an agreement that provided for its repayment in wool. As the wool was to be valued far below the current market price, the merchant got his interest. Rather more crude was the charge of a sum of money for carrying the loan to the borrower. By the end of the thirteenth century Christian merchants were making loans and profiting from them. It is important to notice that to buy a share in a commercial venture was not usury. If you gave a merchant a sum of money and you were to profit or lose according to the success of his venture, it was perfectly proper.

The Place of the Jews

The Jews played an important part in the economic life of the early Middle Ages. In the ninth and tenth centuries they carried on what little trade there was. Then as Christian merchants appeared, the Jews were forbidden to engage in trade. As they were already forbidden to hold land and thus to practice agriculture, they were driven to money-lending. The Jews were completely at the mercy of the lord of the land; they had no rights except what he chose to give them. Many lords considered a colony of Jews a profitable investment. They were allowed to live in the fief under the lord's protection and loan money at interest. Whenever the lord himself needed money, he simply taxed his Jews. In England the king's Jews paid him 10 per cent to help them collect their debts. When a Jew died, a third of his property went to the crown. This represented the regular exploitation. But the king was always free to take anything his Jews had by any means he chose. In short, during the early Middle Ages the Jews performed the function of moneylenders largely for the benefit of the feudal princes. As Christians began to take their place, they became less necessary. During the thirteenth century the Jews were largely expelled from western Europe.

Credit and Money

The twelfth and thirteenth centuries saw the development of a number of important devices connected with commerce. Letters of credit were freely used by King John when sending envoys to Rome. The king's letters would request all merchants to lend the bearer a certain sum of money and promised its repayment at the royal exchequer. Bills of exchange were also used to make payments in foreign lands. In the twelfth century this business was handled chiefly by the great military orders, the Templars and the Hospitalers, as a favor to princes and nobles, but by the thirteenth century merchants were prepared to do it. These centuries also saw the beginning of maritime law. Early in the twelfth century the Italian seamen had adopted a code of maritime law, and by its end the so-called Laws of Oléron were generally accepted in the north.

Coinage, the vital medium of exchange in all commercial operations, developed very slowly. Before the middle of the thirteenth century the only coins minted in the states of western Europe outside Italy were silver pennies. Although the pound of 240 pennies, the shilling of 12 pennies, and the mark of 164 pennies were used as moneys of account, there were no coins to represent them. A few Italian gold coins found their way into northern Europe, but they were comparatively rare. As banks of deposit were not available, one could only keep a reserve of money by hoarding in some form. If this was done extensively, it aggravated the persistent shortage of silver bullion that troubled the period. King John attempted to solve this problem by keeping a large part of his reserve funds in the form of precious stones, and other kings and nobles may well have followed this practice.

Conclusion

THE economic and social structure of western Europe was far different in 1300 from what it had been in 1000. In 1000 there had been no towns in the economic sense, simply occasional groups of dwellings clustered about a cathedral, a monastery, or a noble residence. In 1300 Italy north of Rome was a land of city-states. The nobles who had once ruled the countryside were residents of the towns and formed the upper class of citizens. The rural areas were completely dependent politically on the towns. These towns were for the most part republics or communes. Their form of government varied from a tight aristocracy in Venice to at least theoretical democracy in Florence. In most towns there were political parties that struggled so fiercely for power that it was necessary to import a neutral official, called a *podestà*, to rule. The various towns waged bitter wars against one another by means of professional captains at the head of mercenary troops. At times these captains seized the government of the towns and became tyrants or despots. Thus in 1300 some towns had elected podestas, others despots, and a few were ruled by hereditary princes. In short, political variety and continual internal and external strife marked the Italian cities. But this had not seriously interfered with their economic development. Venice, Genoa, and Pisa were great commercial cities with strong navies that ruled the Mediterranean. The products of the east and of North Africa were carried to Italy by their ships. Spices from the Spice Islands were borne to Alexandria by Moslem traders and there sold to Italian merchants. Other Italians collected cotton and silk at the ports of Syria. The towns of Italy that were not ports had flourishing industries. Although the manufacture of woolen cloth was by far the most important, metal products from Italy were valued all over Europe. The great merchants of Italy were rapidly accumulating more money than they could use in their business and were seeking profitable uses for it. Italian merchants were lending the king of England money in order to persuade him to facilitate their buying of English wool. The wealth of the merchants was also used at home. The towns were adorned with fine public buildings, and the merchants built great houses for themselves. Wealth and the availability of products from all lands permitted the nobles and merchants of Italy to live in luxury and comfort unknown in the west. This wealth and the leisure it made possible was to be an important element in the Renaissance.

The great imperial cities of Germany, those that acknowledged no lord but the emperor, were also city-states and ruled the countryside about them. But while Tuscany and Lombardy were almost entirely covered by the city territories, the lands of the German free cities were mere islands among the territories of the princes. Nevertheless the German cities prospered exceedingly. The towns of North Germany were bound together in the Hanseatic League, which had a navy and trading posts scattered over Europe. The merchants of the Hanse traveled south, crossed the Alpine passes to Italy, and brought home the products available in Venice, Genoa, and Milan. These products they distributed through northern Europe. The great textile towns of Flanders, Antwerp, Bruges, Ghent, and Lille were also extremely rich and prosperous. They bought raw wool from England, Ireland, and other producing regions, manufactured it into cloth, and sold the cloth throughout Europe. Many Italian merchants had agents in Flanders to buy wool and sell the products of Italy and the Orient. These agents were beginning to develop a profitable side line in transferring funds from the north to Italy. This foreign exchange business was soon to develop into general banking activities.

Except for London and Paris, which had 40,000 and 213,-000 inhabitants respectively, the towns of England and France were generally smaller and less wealthy than those of Flanders and Germany. But they played an important part in the economic, social, and political life of the land. A fair part of the revenue of the English king came from export duties on wool, and the towns of England elected representatives to sit with the lords and knights of the shires in Parliament. And men sprung from the merchant class were playing a large part in carrying on the powerful royal governments of the French and English kings. Moreover, the towns supplied a market for agricultural produce and so made possible the sale of the surplus grown by the villagers. Thus the growth of commerce and the development of towns had given western Europe a money economy and a merchant class: a middle class between knights and peasants.

As the towns grew and money economy became more and more prevalent, the feudal and seignorial systems decayed. In the twelfth century the counts of Champagne were granting fiefs that consisted of an annual income in money. The holders swore fidelity and homage and were their vassals, but they were nevertheless hired knights whose pay could be easily stopped. At about the same time English barons were giving fiefs that owed the service of a small fraction of that of a knight—1/10, 1/20, 1/40. Obviously, when the baron called his vassals to arms, the holders of these fiefs could only pay a sum of money. By the thirteenth century the barons of England were either paying the king sums of money to avoid military service or serving with a small band of hired knights. The ordinary rear vassal performed his service by making his lord a money payment. As a rule a vassal rarely actually performed his castle-guard duty but rather paid a fee to compensate his lord. Moreover, the great lords were replacing the vassals who acted as their seneschals, constables, and marshals with hired officials. Although this process of commutation of knightly services was rather slower in France than in England, by the end of the thirteenth century the French kings were giving their vassals a choice of serving in the host or paying a sum of money to avoid service. In short, by 1300 the old personal relations between lord and vassals had disappeared to a great extent. What was left was largely a set of financial obligations.

The changed economic conditions had varying effects on the noble class. The great feudal princes gained in power and resources. They had fairs that yielded them rich returns in money and towns that supplied not only money revenue but men of the middle class to serve as officials. By using his money income to hire officials and soldiers, the great lord could become practically independent of his vassals. But the petty lord ruling a few villages had no such opportunities.

He could perhaps collect some tolls from merchants at a bridge or from peddlers at his village market, but in general the new wealth created by towns and commerce passed him by. His only means of obtaining money income was by selling the produce of his demesne and commuting his peasants' services and rents in kind into money payments. As we have seen, most lords did this. Many even rented out their demesne and did no farming directly. By 1300 a large proportion of the lords in France and England were primarily landlords living on money rents that were fixed in amount. In England the lords were fortunate in one respect: they retained by and large the right to take back into their own hands the tenements held by the peasants. In France as a rule the lord could not dispossess a peasant who paid his rent and fulfilled all his obligations. When inflation began to appear in the fourteenth and fifteenth centuries, the nobles of France found themselves caught between rising costs of living and fixed incomes. The English gentry managed in one way or another to increase their rents as money fell in value and prices rose.

In 1300 then the new economy had made much larger the gap between the great feudal prince and the lesser lords. But until serious inflation began, both groups were benefited. No longer did the petty noble have to wear clothes woven by the unskilled labor of his peasants. He could use his money income to buy rich cloths at the great fairs or at the neighboring town even though he was then dependent on his domestic help to make it into garments. He could enliven his diet with sugar and spices. In short, in 1300 all nobles were living more luxuriously than they had in 1000, and far more expensively. The minor lords were leaving their gloomy towers and building fortified manor houses with more rooms. The great lords were erecting small palaces within the walls of their castles where they could live in princely style.

Nevertheless, it is important to remember that the noble class had lost to some extent its dominant position in society. Many merchants had annual incomes as large as those of the lesser nobles, and they had far more ready money. They could live as luxuriously as could the lords. By serving kings and princes they competed with the nobles for political power. Moreover, the noble had lost his unique position as a soldier. Late in the twelfth century the kings of France and England were using lowborn mercenaries as crossbowmen. By 1300 the bulk of the English army was composed of bowmen and pikemen drafted from the countryside. The nobles still formed the cavalry, but they were no longer the only effective soldiers. In short, although the nobles were to retain for some five centuries more their position at the head of European society, their decline had definitely begun.

The rise of towns and the revival of commerce had affected in many ways the status of the peasant. In the eleventh and twelfth centuries when the growth of towns was extremely rapid, large numbers of peasants had migrated to the towns, with or without the permission of their lords, and had become members of the new middle class, merchants or artisans. By the end of the thirteenth century, however, most towns discouraged such migration. There were enough people in them already to fill the demand for goods and services and new settlers simply lowered the general standard of living. There was always some opportunity for an able and adventurous peasant to advance himself by going to a town, but it became far more difficult to do so successfully. The middle class had been formed and was largely self-propagating.

The peasants who stayed on the land had also been benefited by the revival of a money economy. By 1300 many serfs had bought their freedom, and many free peasants had commuted their services and rents in kind into money payments. As a matter of fact, the commutation of rents and services due from unfree tenants was quite common, especially in England. Commutation was of immediate benefit to the peasant only by giving him greater freedom to dispose of his time and products. He could sell his surplus produce and also his free time. But when inflation began to appear in the fourteenth century, he benefited enormously. His obligations were fixed, and the value of what he raised was increased. This was particularly true when a catastrophe like the Black Death brought a scarcity of labor and hence higher wages. The peasant was still, however, politically helpless against the nobles and middle class. Moreover, he suffered most severely from the wars into which the kings and their nobles continually plunged their realms.

There is no doubt that the population of western Europe increased greatly between the years 1000 and 1300. Once more it is only for England that one can find figures that can be used with any confidence. In 1086 England apparently had a population of 1,100,000 and by 1377 it had 2,230,000 inhabitants. Very rough estimates based on hearth taxes have set the French population at about 16,000,000 in the middle of the fourteenth century, but here we have no figures whatever for the earlier period. But we know that between 1000 and 1300 large areas of new land were brought under cultivation and a considerable urban population added. On the whole it seems likely that the population of western Europe as a whole was larger in 1300 than it was to be again for several centuries. For the Black Death that struck in the middle of the fourteenth century was not a single catastrophe that could be recovered from quickly but an endemic plague that continued its ravages.

The achievements of mediaeval society during the three centuries from 950 to 1250 were very considerable. The peasants had cleared forests, drained swamps, and brought wastelands into cultivation. Vast barren moors once useless had been covered with grazing sheep. Agricultural technique had been improved in important particulars. Improvements in harness allowed two oxen to pull the plows once drawn by eight and in some advanced regions enabled men to use horses for farm work. Wherever the fertility of the soil made it feasible, the three-field had replaced the two-field system. In 1250 northern Europe was supporting a far larger population than it had in any previous period. Meanwhile vigorous and adventurous merchants had built towns and developed a flourishing commerce. Artisans had made great advances in industrial technology, especially in the metal trades and in the making of cloth. The use of the windmill had added to the sources of power at man's disposal. But perhaps the most striking change was in the development of the building crafts. In 950 stone churches were far from numerous, and only a king or very great feudal prince had a stone house. By 1250 every village had its stone church and the monasteries and episcopal cities boasted magnificent Romanesque or Gothic churches. Moreover, every baron of any importance had at least one stone castle and even petty lords lived in strong, well-built moated granges. When one considers the very limited knowledge of labor-saving devices and of engineering techniques, the buildings erected during this period appear as a stupendous achievement.

While the lower classes were following the plow, engaging in trade, mining, making cloth, and building churches and castles, the nobles were perfecting the feudal political and military system. Feudal military organization was on the whole highly effective. The knights of Europe conquered vast territories from the Slavs, pressed the Moslems steadily back in Spain and drove them from Sicily, and established themselves at least temporarily in Palestine, Syria, the Byzantine lands, and Greece. And as a defensive military system feudalism was almost perfect. No organization ever devised could so quickly produce an effective military force wherever it was needed. The feudal army was essentially a militia, but a militia composed of the best soldiers of the day. On the political side feudalism had grave faults. It was not an effective means of keeping order, but it contained elements that were to be extremely important in the future. The feudal class was a ruling aristocracy, but within its own ranks its political ideas were essentially democratic. The fief was ruled more by the vassals than by the lord, and the basic conception of government by mutual agreement —implied in feudal custom—provided the chief justification for later efforts to limit royal authority and has come to be recognized as an important source for the modern conviction that human rights and dignity are safe only within the framework of a constitution.

CHRONOLOGICAL CHART

Country	8th Century	9th Century	10th Century	11th Century	12th Century	13th Century
Italy	Vassalage introduced by Franks	Moslems seize Sicily and raid mainland		Development of towns in Lombardy and Tuscany Appearance of communes Genoa and Pisa aid First Crusade	Lombard League of towns Genoa and Pisa develop active trade with east Textile industry important	Communes become independent Beginnings of banking
France	*Vassi dominici* of Carolingians Beginnings of seignorial system	Viking raids Moslem raids Beginnings of feudalism Spread and growth of seignorial system	End of Viking raids Development of feudal hierarchy Clearing of forest and wasteland	Feudal and seignorial systems fully developed Castles built Towns begin to appear First troubadours Earliest manuscript of Chanson de Roland	Fairs of Champagne Towns spread in northern France Court of Marie de Champagne Tournaments appear Textile industry in Flanders	Freeing of serfs becomes common Craft guilds develop rapidly Lords rent demesnes and become mere rent collectors
England	Commendation well known Seignorial system on some estates Viking raids	Viking raids Danish conquest and unification of Anglo-Saxon state Appearance of thanage		Danish conquest Norman conquest and introduction of feudalism Seignorial system takes Norman form	Towns and trade develop Cistercians start large-scale woolgrowing Extensive commutation of rents and services	Wool becomes chief English export Towns, fairs, markets increase Craft guilds develop
Germany	Frankish conquest of Saxony	Beginnings of feudalism in western Germany	Magyar raids First attempts to colonize beyond river Elbe Clearing of forest and wasteland	Castles built Feudalism spreads into Swabia and Bavaria *Ministeriales* Seignorial system grows rapidly	Successful colonization beyond Elbe Feudalism becomes general Towns grow	Imperial cities rich and powerful Seignorial system spreads to east Beginnings of Hanseatic League

101

Suggestions for Further Reading

THE outstanding recent work on feudalism in its broad sense, that is, covering both the feudal and seignorial systems, is Marc Bloch, *La Société féodale*, 2 vols. (Paris, 1940). There are several briefer works of high quality. J. Calmette, *La Société féodale* (Paris, 1953) covers the same ground as Bloch in shorter space and simpler form. Carl Stephenson, *Mediaeval Feudalism* (Ithaca, N.Y., 1942) and F. L. Ganshof, *Feudalism* (London, 1952) are excellent studies of feudalism in the sense that the term is used in this essay. Bryce Lyon, *From Fief to Indenture* (Cambridge, Mass., 1957) is an important account of the decline of feudal institutions. Sidney Painter, *French Chivalry* (Ithaca, N.Y., 1957) deals with the life and ideas of the feudal class. Although difficult to classify, R. W. Southern, *The Making of the Middle Ages* (New Haven, 1953) is a stimulating essay on the formation of mediaeval society in the eleventh and twelfth centuries and should be mentioned.

Perhaps the best means of understanding the way of life of the feudal class is by reading the literature of the time. The *Chanson de Roland* is available in many translations, but the one by Dorothy L. Sayers in the Penguin Classics is especially readable. There is a good translation of *Raoul de Cambrai* in the Broadway Medieval Library. Although there seems to be no complete English translation of the *Lais* of Marie de France, there are a number of good partial collections. The romances of Chrétien de Troyes can be read in translation in a volume of Everyman's Library.

The first two volumes of *The Cambridge Economic History of Europe* (Cambridge, Eng., 1941, 1952) are standard works for agriculture, trade, and industry in the Middle Ages. P. B. Boissonade, *Life and Work in Medieval Europe* (New York, 1927) is an older comprehensive survey. The seignorial system is covered by the books of Bloch and Calmette mentioned above. The best description of life in an agricultural village is H. S. Bennett, *Life on an English Manor* (Cambridge, Eng., 1938). G. C. Homans, *English Villagers of the Thirteenth Century* (Cambridge, Mass., 1940) is a fascinating study of the same subject from a sociological point of view. Since mediaeval economic conditions were widely localized and diverse, regional studies are of the greatest importance to the student. Two recent examples of such works are Edward Miller, *The Abbey and Bishopric of Ely* (Cambridge, Eng., 1951) for England and Georges Duby, *La Société aux XIe et XIIe siècles dans la région mâconnaise* (Paris, 1953) for France.

A valuable collection of sources and introduction to the importance of mediaeval Mediterranean commerce is R. S. Lopez and I. W. Raymond, *Medieval Trade in the Mediterranean World* (New York, 1955). The best brief study of the rise of towns is Henri Pirenne, *Medieval Cities* (New York, 1956). Carl Stephenson, *Borough and Town* (Cambridge, Mass., 1933) is a more detailed account of English urban institutions. C. E. Petit-Dutaillis, *Les Communes françaises* (Paris, 1947) is the most recent study of French towns.

The practical aspects of mediaeval living such as food, clothing, and shelter are explored in U. T. Holmes, Jr., *Daily Living in the Twelfth Century* (Madison, Wis., 1953). Contemporary works that show the life of other classes than the nobles are rather rare, but anyone who will read Langland's *Piers Plowman* or Chaucer's *Canterbury Tales* will be well rewarded for his effort. They give a glimpse into the minds and lives of simple people that can be gained in no other way.

Index